"*Real Talk about Sex and Consent* is a current and (guage they understand and stories they can relate phors and acronyms makes key concepts about cor and put into action. It is also an invaluable tool fo: the lives of young people who want to have meaningful conversations about this important topic. My stepdaughters will definitely be getting a copy!"

> —**Saleema Noon, BA, MA, OBC**, sexual health educator,
> and coauthor of *Talk Sex Today*

"Written in a way that is honest, informative, and engaging, Cheryl Bradshaw's book, *Real Talk About Sex and Consent*, is an important read for all teenagers, educators, and parents. In order to shift often unsafe societal views around sex and relationships, our young people need to know and understand their rights regarding consent and intimacy. This book provides life-changing information, as well as practical ideas and scenarios so teenagers can feel empowered and safe as they head into adulthood."

> —**Jayneen Sanders**, educator, and author of *Let's Talk About
> Body Boundaries, Consent and Respect*

"This book is timely, inclusive, and incredibly comprehensive. We have been teaching youth about their bodies, relationships, and their sexual health rights for over forty years—and this book effectively addresses their most asked questions and demystifies the topic of consent. This is a great resource for youth and their parents to start the conversation about consent, healthy relationships, and preventing sexual violence. We would highly recommend this book!"

> —**Centre for Sexuality**, organization in Calgary, AB, Canada,
> that has been providing relationship and sexual health education
> to youth in Alberta since 1975

"Cheryl Bradshaw does a deep and important dive into the murky waters of teen sex and consent in her book, *Real Talk about Sex and Consent*. Not only does she bring clarity to the topic, but she also empowers the reader in the process. Cheryl compassionately and effectively guides teens through the basics of sex, communicating with consent, boundaries, alcohol and drugs, and sexual assault. This is a must-read for every teen, parent, caregiver, and educator of teens."

> —**Michelle Skeen, PsyD**, and **Kelly Skeen**, coauthors of *Just As You Are*

"In *Real Talk about Sex and Consent*, Cheryl Bradshaw goes beyond simple slogans and gets to the root of why consent matters. Not only does this book help teens understand what true consent looks and sounds like, it's a compassionate guide that teaches youth to better understand their desires, boundaries, and relationship needs."

—**Nadine Thornhill, EdD**, sexuality educator, speaker, and
cohost of *Every Body Curious*

"*Real Talk about Sex and Consent* targets a deep and painful gap in our understanding of sexual intimacy. With her inviting style, Cheryl Bradshaw goes beyond the yes/no, providing depth and dimension to a topic we have only touched on at a surface level. Every teen should have the opportunity to move through apprehension to greater confidence in communicating needs and developing healthy and more fulfilling relationships. A true gift."

—**Erin Lipsitt, MSW, RSW**, therapist, and mother of two teens

"A ray of hope for our next generation! This book provides a clear and in-depth discourse on sex and consent, and meticulously walks the reader through the 'who, what, when, where, why, and how' of total consent. Bradshaw demystifies the often misunderstood experience of survivors of sexual assault. A crucial read in the time of the #MeToo movement. It's a must-read for teens, parents, counselors, health care practitioners, lawyers, judges, and educators."

—**Kanchan Kurichh Keigher, MA, RP**, registered psychotherapist; Ontario College Counselor at Sheridan College in Oakville, ON, Canada; and yoga teacher

"I spend a lot of time discussing complex and sometimes uncomfortable issues with teens and their families, and I admire the inclusive and accessible language Bradshaw uses to speak to young people. She provides clear and up-to-date information around the use of contraception and protection from sexually transmitted infections. I would recommend this book to teens and anyone who cares for them who is looking to start a conversation about healthy relationships!"

—**Gabrielle Salmers, FRCPC**, general pediatrician

"This book is an easy read that navigates through the fundamentals of consent. Using real examples that are clear and appreciable, the reader can understand consent and all the problematic avenues that an individual may face when applying consent skills. The reader is provided with an opportunity to reflect on the points presented to develop their confidence and values."

—**Lisa Perizzolo, MEd, SHEC**, school counselor, and certified sexual health educator

"Consent is a heavy topic, but there is none more important. *Real Talk about Sex and Consent* provides readers with the knowledge and tools to create their own road map for healthy and fulfilling relationships. Bradshaw offers an in-depth consideration of the many dimensions of consent, and the ways in which it intersects with gender, pleasure, relationships, identity, confidence, communication, and emotional literacy—to name just a few. More than a sex-positive guidebook with real-life examples, it is also packed with practical prompts and scripts for reflection and discussion to engage parents, teens, and partners alike."

—**Jessica O'Reilly, PhD**, sex and relationship expert, host of the *Sex With Dr. Jess* podcast, founder of Happier Couples Inc., and coauthor of *The Ultimate Guide to Seduction and Foreplay*

"The stereotype in media of the approach to intimacy is very real: the assertive party pushing their way to sex through force. From fairy tales to film, many youths have been raised with that vision. In reality, consent is a serious thing. So too, are the legal and personal consequences of failing to obtain it. Bradshaw has created a delicate yet direct guide on this difficult topic—a guide that has long been waited for."

—**Michael R. Larrett, BA (Hons.), JD**, crown Prosecutor for Alberta Crown Prosecution Service Criminal Justice Division

the *i*nstant help solutions series

Young people today need mental health resources more than ever. That's why New Harbinger created the **Instant Help Solutions Series** especially for teens. Written by leading psychologists, physicians, and professionals, these evidence-based self-help books offer practical tips and strategies for dealing with a variety of mental health issues and life challenges teens face, such as depression, anxiety, bullying, eating disorders, trauma, and self-esteem problems.

Studies have shown that young people who learn healthy coping skills early on are better able to navigate problems later in life. Engaging and easy-to-use, these books provide teens with the tools they need to thrive—at home, at school, and on into adulthood.

This series is part of the **New Harbinger Instant Help Books** imprint, founded by renowned child psychologist Lawrence Shapiro. For a complete list of books in this series, visit newharbinger.com.

real talk about
sex & consent

what every teen
needs to know

CHERYL M. BRADSHAW, MA

Instant Help Books
An Imprint of New Harbinger Publications, Inc.

Publisher's Note

NEW HARBINGER PUBLICATIONS is a registered trademark of New Harbinger Publications, Inc.

Distributed in Canada by Raincoast Books

Copyright © 2020 by Cheryl M. Bradshaw
                Instant Help Books
                An imprint of New Harbinger Publications, Inc.
                5674 Shattuck Avenue
                Oakland, CA 94609
                www.newharbinger.com

Cover design by Amy Shoup; Acquired by Elizabeth Hollis Hansen; Edited by Cecilia Santini

Library of Congress Cataloging-in-Publication Data

Names: Bradshaw, Cheryl M., author.
Title: Real talk about sex and consent : what every teen needs to know / Cheryl Bradshaw, RP, MA.
Description: Oakland, CA : Instant Help Books, an imprint of New Harbinger Publications, Inc., [2020] | Series: Instant help solutions
Identifiers: LCCN 2020012131 (print) | LCCN 2020012132 (ebook) | ISBN 9781684034499 (trade paperback) | ISBN 9781684034505 (pdf) | ISBN 9781684034512 (epub)
Subjects: LCSH: Sexual consent--Juvenile literature. | Sex instruction for teenagers.
Classification: LCC HQ35 .B8134 2020 (print) | LCC HQ35 (ebook) | DDC 613.9071/2--dc23
LC record available at https://lccn.loc.gov/2020012131
LC ebook record available at https://lccn.loc.gov/2020012132

Printed in the United States of America

23   22   21

10   9   8   7   6   5   4   3   2

To every survivor of sexual assault, you are strong, you are worthy, you are amazing, and I believe you.

To every educator on the topic of consent, sexual assault, and bystander intervention, thank you for everything you do to help make the world a better and safer place.

To every person who cares about consent, keep it up. We need more people in the world like you.

Contents

Letter to Parents and Educators

First of all, thank you; thank you a thousand times for picking up this book. While I hope that one day everyone will understand true and total consent, we're only just beginning to be properly educated about it. Shifting our cultural and societal awareness starts with parents and educators like you. So thank you for diving into this discussion with the teens in your life, and, hopefully, spreading the word in your communities too!

In the seven years I worked at colleges, I saw multiple approaches to talking about consent with freshmen during orientation weeks. I've seen even more approaches since then in my private practice with teens and parents. I taught a college course called "The Philosophy of Love and Sex," which explored consent and other topics. I've run various workshops on healthy and safe sex and consent for residence programs, and supported consent workshops and activities. But there's even more to do and to cover, which this book explains and expands on.

This book goes past basic definitions of consent to explore the pressures teens face, how they might feel about their own sexuality and readiness, their often confusing schemas and expectations, and the realities of how our bodies and brains respond in sexual encounters. We are going to explore those responses both in encounters where everyone feels safe and we react with enthusiasm, and in encounters where we feel unsafe and we react with fear and various survival instincts. Then we're going to explore what to do about it all: showing teens how to navigate sexual encounters with respect for each other's boundaries and autonomy, and how to have healthy relationships, set boundaries, and deal with rejection.

As you read this book, either with a teen or individually, you can access additional "Consent in Action" exercises on my publisher New Harbinger's website. Just go to http://www.newharbinger.com /44499 and follow the prompts there. You can check out these examples and work through them after you've covered the material in this book to put everything you've read into practice.

There is also an online video-series course that can accompany this book for those who want extra guidance and structure and to support various learning styles. You can find the link to this course at http://www.cherylmbradshaw.com.

And most of all, if I can ask one thing of you, it's to share this book and what you learn with other parents. There is valuable information here—about boundaries, reciprocity, respect, how the brain and body work in times of stress and pressure, and how to handle the complexity of sexual intimacy—information that all teens need to know in order to bring about a healthier and safer future for everyone. We can only do this if we all keep learning and we all keep talking.

I look forward to working through this book with you and your teen!

Consent:
Welcome to the Conversation!

Welcome, dear reader! I'm so glad you're here. We're going to talk about some pretty big things in this book. There's going to be a lot to learn and a lot to unpack. It's so important that you're reading this right now. Because a generation that truly understands sex and consent could really change the world.

You can be a sexually empowered generation, champions for a safety that previous generations haven't had access to. You can be a generation of people who feel like they have the ability, knowledge, and skills to communicate about consent confidently, caringly, and respectfully. You have so much potential, and a better shot at achieving this than anyone before you! You can build a new model of how to interact and be intimate with each other that could be more powerful, connected, and healthy than ever before. You can even help educate the adults you know too.

Sex can be a fun, awesome, and exciting part of your life once you decide you're ready, if it's something you want to be a part of your life. But it all hinges on the idea of consent. Sexy moments are only awesome if everyone involved feels safe and fully "into" them. Each person should want to be a part of every part of a sexual situation: the who, what, when, where, why, and how of sex and sexual intimacy. That's consent. For everyone to feel empowered in sexual situations, there needs to be active, clear, enthusiastic agreement (yes, please!) from everyone to participate in a sexual act.

Being intimate with others safely and considerately shows people that they're worthy and respected, which everyone deserves. And you can also feel empowered when you're treating yourself and others with respect and consideration. By doing this, your relationship with *yourself* will grow too!

INFORMATION IS POWER

Sex can be fascinating, wonderful, exciting, liberating, and fantastic—but it can also feel a bit overwhelming and nerve-wracking at times. Sometimes knowing what to do or what to say can feel confusing. What does consent look like? How do we know if we truly have consent? How do we handle moments when we don't want to do something? How do we know if our partners want to do something with us or not?

If we don't know what consent looks like and sounds like and how to handle the confusion and mixed feelings that can come up, we could go into sexual encounters unprepared. If this happens, we risk doing real emotional or psychological damage to our partners and to ourselves. On the other hand, when we *do* practice consent properly, we're empowered. We know our rights and we have the strength to make them clear to our partners. And our partners are also empowered when we respect their rights too.

Sex has a big impact on our emotions and our bodies, so it's important to approach it with good information and in the best way that we can. We want to feel empowered and for our partners to feel that way too. And we want everyone to feel safe, so that we can truly enjoy healthy sexual experiences!

Taking Care of Yourself as You Read This Book

Consent is so important. It has to do with our safety in intimate moments. We're going to be exploring some heavy topics as we move through this book. One of those topics is sexual contact that happens without a person's consent, which is known as *sexual assault*. Another tough topic is *trauma,* which can be caused by sexual assault. Trauma is an intense emotional reaction people have in the aftermath of bad things happening to them.

If you've had personal experiences of being unsafe or having bad things happen in your life, some parts of this book may be difficult to read. They may remind you of certain events in your own life, which could bring up some intense or overwhelming emotions for you.

If you have been through something painful like this, first of all, I want you to know that whatever happened, it wasn't your fault. I hope with all my heart that you have someone you can talk to about it and get support from, because you deserve it.

If you haven't talked to anyone about it yet, you haven't done anything wrong. You're doing the best you can. But I want you to know that *you are worthy and you deserve support,* if and when you're ready. You are worth taking care of, and there are safe people out there who will be there for you and listen to you. And know that no matter what you choose to do or how you choose to proceed with getting support, I am sending you love and strength. I believe you.

So if parts of this book are difficult to read or triggering, let's make a quick plan on how you can take care of yourself as you work through it. If you start to feel overwhelmed at any point as you read, you might put the book down for the day. Take some deep breaths. Do some things that bring you back to the present moment and into your body, away from the thoughts and memories that started to feel overwhelming. Go for a walk, call a friend, play with a pet, get some exercise, or do some hobbies you enjoy. Talk to friends or family to help rebalance.

Take things at a pace you're comfortable with, and know that your physical and mental health is always the first priority. Slow down or take space if you need to.

You can also call a local mental health helpline in your area for additional support if you don't yet feel comfortable talking to friends or family about what you're going through. Take a moment and look up a number in your area, and jot it down in the space below. Then you can come back to this number any time you need it:

Name of Helpline: _____

Helpline Phone #: _____

Once you have a sense of what your supports are and how to take time out if you need to, let's keep working ahead together.

WHY THIS BOOK

In my work as a therapist, I talk to young people about their sexual experiences all the time: the good experiences, and, unfortunately, the not-so-good experiences too. And I've come to realize how often we're confused about our own brains, bodies, and reactions—especially where sex is concerned.

The stories I hear in counseling sessions come from people who are confused about what happened, why it happened the way it did, and why they didn't react differently in the moment. Many of the stories I've heard have similar themes.

One young woman told me how she had ended up at the house of a man she met at a bar one night. She didn't know exactly where she was. As she realized that she didn't want to have sex with the man, she offered him oral sex instead, even though she didn't want to do that, either. The young woman told me that she was confused why she had reacted this way. Why didn't she just run, say no, or leave the situation? I didn't have the answer at the time—all I knew was that it wasn't her fault, and I told her this. It wasn't. It is *always* the responsibility of the person initiating the sexual experience to ensure they have full, total consent. But I struggled with the same question as she did. Why did this response happen, instead of the one she expected; why didn't she say no or ask to leave when she didn't want to be there?

I heard another story from a young man who was upset his girlfriend had broken up with him for cheating on her. But he said the situation was more complicated than that. Another woman he knew had come to his apartment after a night of heavy drinking. She insisted that he have sex with her. He asked her to leave, but she wouldn't, and she continued to ask him for sex, which eventually happened. His girlfriend found out and broke up with him. But this young man hadn't given true consent; he was cornered and pressured after he said no. He was confused as he told me his story too. He thought he'd deserved to lose his girlfriend, and that he was weak for not refusing to have sex with the other woman. He blamed himself completely—but it wasn't his fault either. And the question of how and why this happened remained a mystery to him too. Why did sex happen when he didn't truly want it?

I heard versions of both of these stories multiple times. And I began thinking of my own life and my own experiences. I've lived through some of these confusions and difficult situations myself. When I was in school, for instance, at all-ages dances, boys would come up behind my group of female friends and start dancing or grinding behind us without asking. And my friends and I would never tell them whether we were or weren't okay with this. Instead, we came up with a "code" of facial expressions so we could "save" each other if we didn't like what was happening. And it just felt so normal. Even though something didn't feel right about it, I came to assume that was just the way it had to be, and life carried on.

This pattern—don't say what you want or don't want, just get away without making a scene—ended up being the theme of several encounters again even in college. There, when a boy I'd met during freshman week wanted to dance, I agreed, as a friend—I was in a relationship with someone else. After a little while, he leaned in to kiss me. I pulled back and reminded him I had a boyfriend. He tried to talk me into it anyway. I kept pushing him away, "playfully," gig-gling, as I made an excuse to get away. Eventually, I had to hide in the bathroom until I could find my friends. When I told them about his behavior, they weren't concerned. Instead, they were impressed that I'd been so aggressively pursued. What a compliment! Again, I thought maybe this was just how the world was. But it didn't feel right. Why had he kept going, when I'd told him I had a boyfriend, when I'd given him so many signs it wasn't okay? Why did it feel so hard to be firm and clear about what I didn't want?

During my third year, a male friend walked me home from a bar after a night out with friends. When we got to my front door, he asked to kiss me, and I said that it wasn't a good idea. I was friendly and playful about it, trying to keep things light; after all, he was my friend. He asked a few more times. I kept saying no, but I was gig-gling as I tried to figure out why he still had his arm around me and was still asking me. And then he kissed me anyway. I didn't slap him like they do in the movies. It appeared that I let it happen in the moment and then walked calmly through my front door, even though I was twisted up inside. I slept badly. When I woke up the next day I cried.

In my early twenties, a much older male supervisor drove me to an abandoned parking lot after we had dinner. He asked to kiss me, leaning in, not waiting for an actual answer. I was pretty much stuck—in a car, in an abandoned parking lot that I didn't ask to go to—and there weren't a whole lot of options. It wasn't a safe place. I didn't scream, or hit, or kick, or yell for help, even though that's what I had been taught to do. Instead, I watched myself as if from outside my body, kissing him back until it was over and he agreed to drive me back to my car.

When I was safely back at home, I threw up, cried, and called my boyfriend. I felt so confused. Why did this keep happening to me? Why did I giggle and laugh my way through these situations when I had always been told to scream, push, yell, or run? Why couldn't I seem to access the tough, assertive part of me that I always imagined when I pictured this kind of thing? Where was my kung fu ninja kick to the groin I'd planned? Why would my body seem to undermine what I was saying by giggling or not being assertive? My body didn't act like I was in an emergency when I was in the middle of these situations. This wasn't what I was taught to expect. Something was being lost in translation.

Perhaps there are more nuances to consent than many of us have been taught: important things that can affect our ability to feel safe with each other and our ability to understand and say what we do or don't want.

We're taught certain rules of consent—like "no means no" (it does!)—but we don't always understand on a deeper level what consent *really* looks like and sounds like. That can leave us with questions, and that uncertainty can lead to cutting corners. We may not understand what the harm is in asking for intimacy or sex a few times. We may not understand what the harm is in a few drinks, or coming on a bit strong, or "just making a move." And we may end up believing our ability to read body language is better than it really is—instead of actually asking a person for consent.

Many people believe that if a situation was "really that bad" or if someone "really didn't want it," they would yell, scream, hit, push, or just say no, firmly and forcefully. We might think that it's obvious by a person's reaction when a line is being crossed. And when someone doesn't see this reaction from another person—or sees giggling, joking, or laughing, or the person "giving in" but not being mad—they might assume these messages mean something entirely different than what they actually mean.

And this misinterpretation can affect both how we look for consent and how we give consent to each other. We need to all be speaking the same language. We need to understand ourselves, our bodies, and our brains better. And so in this book, we're going to learn the entire language and process of consent. Because when we know better, we can do better—for ourselves and our partners. Consent is empowerment!

INCLUSIVITY AND DIVERSITY

We're going to explore perspectives for all potential partners, all genders, and all orientations. This book includes language and examples from multiple experiences. While you may see certain genders, orientations, and relationships referenced in scenarios, this doesn't mean the scenario is limited to those specific genders, orientations, and relationships. Remember that consent is a must for all people in all situations in which we're sexually intimate. Consent needs to happen between any and all people involved in a sexual situation.

So, dear reader, let's get started. Let's start pulling apart this whole puzzle, and putting it back together. Because once you know what really goes on inside of us and all the different aspects that come together to create true and total consent, it can make intimate situations so much easier to understand and to navigate. And it can help you make your relationships and your sexual life truly empowering!

To start off, let's take a look at the big questions. What *is* consent, anyway? For that matter, what is sex? When we talk about sex and intimacy, what exactly do we mean?

CHAPTER 1

Sex and You

Maybe you've already started to explore sex and sexuality, or maybe you're not sure about what you want or don't want to explore yet. Different people start to explore sex and sexuality at different ages. Any level of interest in sex—whether a lot or hardly any—is okay and normal! Wherever you are on this spectrum, know that there is no "right" and no "wrong"—provided everyone is safe and respectful, of course.

You shouldn't feel guilty or ashamed for being interested in sex, or for wanting to explore this part of yourself and your life. You also shouldn't feel guilty or ashamed for not wanting to explore these things yet, or ever, or not feeling ready to.

If you are curious about sex and sexuality, there are lots of ways to explore your body, your feelings, your emotions, and your preferences on your own. This is a great and safe place to start. However, many people do eventually decide they would like to explore these feelings and experiences with a trusted partner. This is where consent comes into the picture.

There are as many different opinions, ideas, and beliefs about sex and sexuality as there are people in this world. So, the main thing to know as we explore consent is that *your body and your decisions are up to you.* This is the basis of consent—that you get to be in charge of the decisions you make with your body, in every way: the who, what, when, where, why, and how of being sexually intimate with someone. Your partner should also feel respected in this same way. They should also feel in control of the who, what, when, where, why, and how of their choice to be sexually active or intimate.

Let's explore the basics of where this all starts: sex! What are we referring to in this book when we talk about sex and sexual acts?

SEX: THE BASICS

The word *sex* can mean so many different things to so many different people. When we use that word in this book, we're referring to the broad spectrum of sexual experiences that people may have. Sex is basically any kind of activity you're engaging in, by yourself or with someone else, that is intimate in nature, usually involving the genital area. It can mean vaginal sex, anal sex, oral sex, or other forms of genital stimulation with hands or other body parts.

We'll also use terms like "sexual intimacy" or "intimacy" for short. Because when we're talking about consent, we want to look at all types of intimacy, as each one requires consent from another person—whether cuddling on a couch, kissing or making out, or other forms of sexual intimacy. No matter how big or small, every form of intimacy requires consent from everyone involved.

Every time we engage with another person in a sexually intimate way, consent needs to be part of the picture. And consent isn't just a question and answer. It isn't just someone asking, "Do you want to…?" and someone else answering with "yes" or "no." **Consent is a complete way of approaching sexual intimacy from the ground up.** In this book, we're going to explore *total* consent: the total consent of mind, body, and spirit with both verbal language and body language communication, with each partner feeling in control of every aspect of the experience.

While starting to explore sex and sexuality with others can be exciting for many people, it actually helps to start with getting to know yourself first! No matter who you might start to explore your sexuality with, *you* are, of course, always going to be part of the interaction. So getting to know yourself *before* bringing another person into the equation can help you feel more clear about your likes, dislikes, wants, desires, boundaries, and readiness for certain activities or relationships.

If we take the time to get to know ourselves better, this can make it much easier to communicate about consent with a partner. Once we are more clear in our own minds about who we are and what we want—and don't want—we can use that as a guidepost to start thinking about consent. And at any point in your sexual life, you can revisit these next questions as you grow, evolve, and experience new things. So let's take a look at the first part of the equation of your sexual life: you!

WHO ARE YOU? WHAT DO YOU WANT?

Let's look at a few things you may want to consider about yourself and your relationship with yourself and with sex. Some of these questions will ask you to start thinking about ideas such as your gender (how masculine or feminine you may feel—or if you feel that way at all) and your sexuality (what genders or types of people you feel sexually attracted to, if any), and the types of relationships you may or may not be interested in right now, or ever. We will also explore how ready you feel for emotional or physical intimacy, and how comfortable you are right now with setting boundaries about what is and isn't okay for you.

Read through the following questions and see what comes up for you as you consider them. Keep in mind that these questions can often be complex, even for many adults. But they're important to consider, no matter your age. Whatever you feel as you think about them—excited, intimidated, curious, overwhelmed—know that there are no wrong answers.

If it helps, you can grab a pen and paper to jot some of your ideas down. You can also jot down any questions these ideas bring up for you that you may want to learn more about later.

Also know that this is only a snapshot of where you are right now. Some of your answers might change as you get older or after you have different experiences, and that's okay! All of this is just to get you started thinking about sex and intimacy: how you feel about it, and what you might want or not want, at least for right now.

Gender Identity and Sexuality

- How do you see your gender identity and your sexual preferences, at this point in time?

    If you're not sure where to start with this question, look up the Genderbread Person, at genderbread.org (Killermann

2017). It shows the different aspects of gender identity and expression really well. It explains some of these terms:

- There are many different gender identities recognized around the world. Common ones include transgender, cis-gender, and nonbinary.

  "Transgender" or "trans" refers to when a person's true gender is different than the one assigned to them at birth. "Cisgender" refers to when a person's gender is the same as the one assigned to them at birth. "Nonbinary" refers to a person whose gender doesn't fall within the male-female binary. A nonbinary person might see themselves some-where between "male" or "female" or somewhere else entirely.

    - **Gender expression:** This is how you present your gender through your clothing, actions, and demeanor, and where those presentations are viewed along a mas-culinity and femininity spectrum, if at all.

    - **Anatomical sex:** This is your physical sex, as male (e.g., penis, testicles), female (e.g., vagina, ovaries), or inter-sex (not fitting the traditional physical definitions of male or female bodies), and your sex characteristics, and how these may change over time. Anatomical sex is on a spectrum of female-ness and male-ness, if at all. There are at least five different anatomical sexes.

    - **Attraction:** Attraction is felt in your heart. Being attracted to someone is wanting to be either romantic or sexual with that person, or both. You can be attracted to people of all genders, some genders, or only a specific gender, with a range of masculinity or femininity, or not be attracted to anyone at all.

Keep in mind that everything is on a spectrum. And remember that identity doesn't equal expression, which doesn't equal sex, and gender isn't the same as sexual orientation. These terms are each different and independent of each other. A person can be many combinations or expressions of any of these aspects, or none at all.

So where do you feel you fit right now in your life?

- Given the above definitions, how do you feel about your own gender identity, gender expression, anatomical sex, and attraction to others? Where do you see yourself on each of these spectrums?

- Do you have certain pronouns you feel more aligned with that describe your gender (like he, she, them, or another pronoun)?

Relationships

- What types of intimate relationships are you looking for at this point in your life, if any? Let's look at a few common types of relationships:

  - **Exclusive/monogamous relationships:** These types of relationships involve two people that agree to only date each other and to only be sexually intimate with each other. Every couple may be different on the exact things they are comfortable doing or not doing within their specific relationship, and these things can always be discussed and agreed upon together.

- **Abstinent relationships:** In these types of relationships, the partners aren't sexual with each other. They might be waiting until a later time to have sex, or they may have decided not to be sexual at any point. Partners may or may not be physically and sexually attracted to each other, but they choose to only have romantic interactions and not sexual interactions.

- **Casual intimacy or casual sex relationships:** In these relationships, two or more people may meet up for sex without the expectation of romantic involvement. These relationships may be more recreational than emotional in nature.

- **Friends with benefits:** These are friendships between two people who agree to remain "just friends" in terms of emotional closeness and commitment, but are sexually intimate when they are both in the mood—sometimes exclusively with each other, but sometimes not.

- **Open relationships:** These relationships usually involve two romantic and sexual partners who agree that they can have sex with other partners as well as each other. However, the original relationship remains "primary," and partners usually agree that romantic or emotional relationships aren't acceptable outside the "primary" relationship.

• **Polyamorous relationships:** In these relationships, a person has more than one romantic partner or relationship at a time. Many polyamorous people have one "primary" partner and one or more "secondary" partners. But many polyamorous people also have simultaneous, equal relationships with more than one person, sharing closeness and connection among multiple people. Often, there may be groups of three or more who share relationships and intimacy equally between all partners.

It's clear there are many different types of relationships. All of them are valid. But keep in mind that some of these relationship dynamics can be challenging to manage emotionally. They can be challenging even for adults. Emotions and sexual intimacy go together quite naturally, and it can be hard to separate them, even for experienced people. Think about what you feel ready for, and what will work for you and your chosen partner(s).

And at the end of the day, remember: whatever intimate relationships you find yourself exploring, do your best to be open and honest about what you want. Try to be aware if there are pressures or influences on you to act or be a certain way that you may not actually feel comfortable with deep down. And if a particular kind of relationship isn't what you want, it's totally okay not to pursue it.

Emotional Intimacy

- What kind of emotional intimacy (trust and openness with your emotions and personal stuff) feels most comfortable for you right now in a relationship, if you are considering one? Ask yourself these questions:

  - How open do you want to be with a partner about yourself? What types of emotional details do you feel comfortable sharing with another person (like fears, embarrassing stories, and vulnerable topics)? What do you want to keep private right now?

  - How will you know when, or if, you're ready to share new things or trust someone with more emotional information about yourself?

  - How close would you want to be with a partner emotionally? How often would you like to talk or hang out?

- How do you imagine wanting to treat a partner? How would you like to be treated in return?

Sex and Sexual Activity

- What do you know about how physical sexual intimacy works? Are you comfortable with your anatomy, the anatomy of the people you might be interested in, and how it's all supposed to work?

- What would you still like to know about sexual intimacy?

- Are there resources to help you find answers to any questions you have?

- Which **nonphysical** sexual activities are you open to or do you want to experience at this point in time, if any? Nonphysical activities include things like:
  - Using or watching porn, alone or with a partner
  - Reading erotica (written pornography)
  - Talking to a partner about personal fantasies
  - Hearing from a partner about their fantasies
  - Phone sex/virtual sex (not in person)

- What **physical** sexual activities are you open to or do you want to experience at this point in time, if any, with a partner who also feels ready? Sexual physical activities include things like:
  - Holding hands
  - Hugging or cuddling
  - Kissing or making out
  - Grinding or dry humping (rubbing your genital areas together with clothes on)
  - Giving or receiving oral sex
  - Giving or receiving digital sex (using fingers or hands on genitals)
  - Giving or receiving vaginal sex
  - Giving or receiving anal sex

- And for each of the above **nonphysical** and **physical** sexual activities:

  - Which activities do you *not* want to try or experience right now, or maybe ever?

  - Which ones are you kind of interested in at some point, but maybe you do not feel ready for quite yet?

  - Under what circumstances might you want to experience those things that you *do* feel ready for? Do you want to be in a relationship, or in love, or is there some other circumstance you imagine feeling right for you? (Again, all experiences and desires are valid. At the same time, it's important to be sure that they're *your* desires—not the result of pressure of some kind.)

Boundaries and Rejection

Boundaries are our "line in the sand." We set them when we decide what's okay for us and what's not okay for us. When we think about what types of relationships and activities we're comfortable with, we should think about how to set boundaries. We also want to think about how we might deal with disappointment if our desires or feelings aren't returned by someone else. This can be tough to handle even for experienced adults, so let's stop and take a minute to think about where you're starting from:

- How comfortable do you currently feel in expressing boundaries, saying no, or turning down someone? If you can, rate your comfort level on a scale of 1 to 10. On this scale,

1 would be discomfort with setting and expressing boundaries (if you're thinking something like *I don't even think I could get the words out of my mouth, I'd feel so bad*), and 10 would be extreme confidence with your boundaries (being kind to someone, but firm and true to yourself without hesitation). Again, just take note of how you currently feel. And, if your rating is a little low, think about what you can do to try to move up the scale a bit. (We'll talk more about this later too.)

- How comfortable do you currently feel experiencing rejection or disappointment in your life? Rate it on a scale of 1 to 10, if you can. On this scale, 1 would be an expectation of not handling rejection well (if you're thinking something like *It'd literally be the worst and I could barely stand it at all*) and 10 would be feeling confident and in control of your emotions and reactions, even when things are tough. Just take note of how you currently feel. And if your rating is a little low, think about what you can do to try to help move up the scale a bit. (We'll talk more about this later too.)

All of these questions can be pretty complex! You may not know exactly how to answer each of them yet. And that's okay. Just beginning to think about these concepts is a great starting place. And we will keep building on these ideas throughout the book. But for now, as you think about your current orientation to self, sexuality, relationships, emotions, and boundaries, let's also take a moment to think about what influences those ideas.

We're constantly surrounded by all sorts of messages about sex and sexuality—some that are good, but some that are unhealthy too. We often absorb these messages without even realizing it. It's kind of like when you hear a song over and over again. Even if you don't like the song, you eventually learn the lyrics. It can happen unconsciously.

In fact, there's a word for these messages that we absorb from the world around us: *schemas.* Schemas are the simplified, preprogrammed scripts and ideas we have about the world. Related ideas get grouped together in our minds. Like how when you think of going to the movies, you probably think of popcorn and movie trailers too.

The problem is, sometimes the world around us groups ideas together *for* us in ways that aren't exactly healthy. But they get stuck in our heads, just like those lyrics. This happens a lot around the topic of sex. And if we don't notice the ways that these messages may be mixed up, these schemas we form can impact our behavior in not-so-great ways. Let's spend some time sorting out all these influences and ideas, whether helpful or not so helpful, so we can see how they work in our lives.

MYTHS AND INFLUENCES

In this section, we'll explore some of the messages we receive from our families, the media, our peers, and more. We'll consider which messages might be aligned with true consent—remember, consent is full choice over how sex and sexual intimacy is happening, including what, with whom, when, where, and why—and which ones might be leading us astray. Because when we can separate fact from fiction about consent, we can make the best choices for true and total consent with our partners.

From Your Family and Culture

We get various messages from our family and culture about what sex is and what it's all about. When these messages are fairly balanced and healthy, it's great! We're raised with the understanding that sex is a normal and good thing, something that can be a healthy part of life and that we'll enjoy when we've reached the appropriate age or life stage—if we find ourselves interested in exploring it. And when we have questions about sex, we often have people in our lives who can responsibly answer those questions.

But sometimes, our families and cultures are less open about sexual intimacy. Maybe the people you grew up with don't talk much about sex at all. They may let your teachers and sex-ed courses handle the discussion and teach you what you need to know. Often, these school courses do a fine job of covering most of the basics. But sometimes, they can also leave more personal questions unanswered. And sometimes, even if you *are* in a culture or family that's open about sex, it can be hard to know what to ask, where to start, or even how to know what you don't know.

No matter what, it helps to think about and be aware of where some of your earliest messages about sex and sexuality came from to get perspective on what's influenced how you think about sex. Jot a few ideas down, using this set of questions to help you understand your family and cultural influences, both positive and/or negative:

1. What have your culture and family taught you about sex? Facts, emotions, values, or otherwise?

2. What are things you have learned from family or culture that feel important to consider when you think about yourself as a sexual person, and what you want your life to look like?

3. What values and morals feel important to you, personally, that you may have learned from your family?

4. Is there anything about the messages from your family or culture that concerns you and that you want to address or understand better, maybe by talking to another trusted adult or resource?

5. Is there anything you want to ask your family about, or anything about your culture you want to learn, to help you understand yourself or these ideas better?

Whatever the answers to these questions happen to be, remember that no one culture or family is necessarily "better" than any other. The important thing is that everyone is treated with respect. The key is to know that whatever messages you may have received, shame and guilt are not part of healthy sexual development. You don't need to feel guilty or ashamed about sex. Sex and sexuality are normal and natural parts of being human. And as long as you aren't hurting anyone else or yourself, there are no wrong answers about what's right for you.

Ultimately, what's most important is how and why you make decisions. It's important that you feel free and empowered to explore your own life and your own choices about the things you want to do when you're ready. And being able to give and receive consent is a vital part of being able to explore your sexuality in a healthy way.

If you struggle to talk with your family about sex and sexuality, or it doesn't feel safe to do so, seek out resources for support and information, and talk to other adults you can trust, like a teacher, guidance counselor, or therapist.

Outside of our family values, beliefs, and approaches to sex and sexuality, we also hear and see a lot of other messages from the rest of society, the media (like TV, movies, and ads), and our peers.

From Society and the Media

For better or for worse, the way sexual stories and situations are portrayed in the shows we watch or the ads we see can influence the schemas we form about sexual intimacy. We can also be impacted by the way our peers and other people talk about sex and sexual intimacy. These messages can impact how our brain is programmed to think and react in our first sexual situations. And these messages can have this influence even if we're not aware of it.

In fact, these influences are often most overpowering when we're *not* aware of them. But we can work to understand the ideas about sex and intimacy that we've absorbed from the world around us. Then we can help our brain stay updated with what we *truly* believe. The first step is understanding it all.

So, let's look at some of these myths and break them down.

Myth: "This Is What Guys Do, This Is What Girls Do"

In our society, we're often surrounded by gendered stereotypes about the way "guys" behave and the way "girls" behave. Despite the fact that there is no one dynamic for any gender or orientation, a stereotypical male and female dynamic is presented to us over and over again. We are shown and told that "guys" do one thing, and "girls" do another.

These stereotypes are limited to a gender binary (male and female) that doesn't really reflect reality—as we learned, gender is a spectrum, and a lot of people have identities that don't fit in the binary at all. So, a binary (male/female only) approach doesn't reflect reality, and it *also* leaves us with some really sexist ideas about what is and isn't okay for people to do, based on their gender.

In reality, gender shouldn't define our sexuality and expression. What's truly most important is how we want to express our gender and sexuality and, in sexual situations, the consent of whoever we're interacting with. Sometimes stereotypes, like the ones below, don't prioritize consent. This, of course, can be a dangerous way for any of us to think about sex and sexuality.

So let's dive deeper and look at some of the common "guy/girl" messages that don't line up with consent, so we can break apart myth from fact:

- **Guys chase. Girls are chased and won over.** The idea that a person can be "won over" like a prize or an object suggests that only one person's desires (in this case, the guy's) are important, and the goal in sex is to override another person's choices (in this case, the girl's).

If someone isn't interested, "chasing" isn't okay. No one should try to force another person to think or feel a certain way when that person has expressed that they're not interested. We should respect each person's decisions about their own rights and preferences, be kind, and move on. You can of course still be friends with that person—but you shouldn't make it your mission to try to change their mind. Otherwise, consent isn't present—you're trying to override someone else's will and rights with your own agenda, goals, and desires. This kind of aggressive pursuit isn't normal or okay. And to continue to pursue someone who has expressed that they aren't interested is called *harassment*.

- **Guys get sex; girls give it.** This is a similar message to the first one, with the same generalizations about "who does what." Again, it assumes that girls will be passive in their romantic lives, waiting to be approached. And it assumes, again, that guys will be the ones who chase, who always want sex, and who might do any number of things—plead, persuade, or pressure—to get what they're after.

  In fact, many different dynamics can happen between people of all genders—one person may take the lead in suggesting intimacy in one relationship, and sometimes that same person will be in the other role in a different relationship. These dynamics can also shift between people during the course of a relationship. It doesn't really matter who is in which role—the person suggesting intimacy, or the person considering a suggestion. What matters is that all parties are communicating about it with respect and with consent at the forefront.

This message also assumes that sex is something to be traded between people. In reality, sex is something to be *shared* between people. It shouldn't be seen as an expression of power—whether that's a girl's power to grant sex or a guy's power to get it—and it shouldn't be seen as something that one person "owes" another person. Sex and intimacy are shared with consent, because all parties involved *want* to share it, and for no other reason.

- **Guys always want sex.** We often receive messages that guys are considered "lucky" when someone wants to have sex with them. Many guys are shamed or made fun of if they don't pursue sex or accept opportunities to have sex. But in reality, every person is entitled to their own ideas about what they want and when—no matter their gender. Everyone's preferences may differ individually in a way that has nothing to do with gender. Consent is important for *everyone* of all genders and orientations. Everyone has a right to decide what they do and don't want.

- **He's teasing you. That means that he likes you.** This is a message we often get in childhood, like in a situation where a boy is teasing, chasing, or pulling on a young girl's hair. That girl is often unfortunately told that "he just likes you!"

  Experiences like these can teach girls, from a very young age, that to be chased or picked on against their will is "cute," or desirable, which isn't healthy. And it can teach boys that teasing and intruding on someone's personal space is an acceptable way to show how you feel. But this behavior isn't healthy. It's actually harassment. And it can lay the groundwork for pretty toxic patterns in the future—both for girls who may learn that this type of pursuit is okay, and for guys who may think this is a normal way to show affection or attraction.

- **She's a tease. She's leading you on.** Messages like this suggest that one action implies consenting to another—for instance, that if a girl is flirting, it implies that she's going to have sex with the person she's flirting with. It suggests that it's not okay if something physical doesn't follow the flirting—which isn't consent. It also suggests that a girl is not allowed to flirt if she isn't going to do something physical, which also isn't true. Each person can decide exactly how much or how little they would like to do with another person. There are no requirements from anyone, at any time, to have to do anything more than they're doing. Just because one activity is engaged in with consent doesn't mean any other activity needs to follow it. Every activity requires its own consent, and one thing doesn't imply another. Flirting doesn't mean consent to kissing; and kissing doesn't imply consent to oral sex; and so on.

  This is related to the phrase *friendzone*. People say that someone (usually a guy in the stereotype) is friendzoned when they are romantically or sexually interested in a friend (usually a girl) who wants to be friends and nothing beyond that. (Of course, while the friendzone often features a male/

female dynamic, the discussion can apply to any combination of genders.)

The problem with the friendzone discussion is that it implies that friendship between a guy and a girl that doesn't involve sex is inevitably disappointing to the guy. But if someone is just waiting around for their friend to have sex with them rather than valuing their actual friendship, they're really not much of a friend to begin with.

In fact, if a girl, or whoever else, doesn't want to be romantically or sexually involved with a friend, they're simply exercising their right to choose their romantic and sexual partners, and communicating that choice. Everyone has this freedom to decide this. And it's not a bad thing if someone exercises this right—it's a *good* thing! We should all respect each other's preferences and choices.

- **Sex is a "score" or a "goal" for guys.** Guys are often made to feel that a high number of sexual partners is a point of pride—or that a low number is a point of shame. The idea that sex is a goal is often reinforced in our language too. Sometimes this happens in ways that seem so normal that we forget that it's not okay. For instance, there are words like "scoring," "banging," "nailing," and "slaying" and phrases like "home run" or "closing the deal" that can make it seem like sex is an aggressive competition, like something to achieve, rather than something that happens between consenting people. And phrases like "body count," "kill count," or "notches in your belt," which are used to describe how many sexual partners a person has had, can create a belief that sex is a conquest or a game. When we think of having sex with a person as "conquering" that person, we turn humans into objects. This language can make consent, and our partners, seem less important than the quest for sex itself.

At the end of the day, sexual intimacy is about humans coming together freely and openly, because they want to— not for any other reason or "goal." And of course, every person is entitled to their own choices about what feels right for them, and their partner is entitled to that same choice, no matter their gender. There is no "should" and no "right" and no "wrong," for any gender.

Myth: Sex in Real Life Is Like Sex in Movies, TV, and Ads

This is another myth that can seem quite believable at first glance, if we forget to be smart consumers of what we see and hear in the media. It can be easy to assume that what we see is how things should go in real life, because at times, it can just seem so real and so normal. But we do need to think twice about what we hear and see in movies, TV, ads, and other places (even books!), because, unfortunately, they can carry a lot of unhealthy messages about sex and sexuality. The media can often reinforce a lot of the beliefs we just explored above ("This is what guys do, this is what girls do").

Think of the plotlines of so many romances and romantic comedies: guy wants girl, girl turns guy down, guy does something spectacular to win her over, and girl eventually realizes she wanted him all along as he presses her against the wall and kisses her (often initially against her will until she realizes they have chemistry and then falls madly in love with him). See if you can take a moment right now and think of a few movies, shows, or books you've seen or read with this kind of plot!

The other problem with many movies and TV shows is that they'll often simplify and glaze over moments of consent. The characters just "know" when to make a move—but they never discuss it with each other to get real consent. This can make us think that it isn't romantic or normal to ask for someone's consent in an intimate moment. That we should all just "know" without talking about anything with our partners. But it's actually crucial—and normal!—to have these conversations. In real life, where no one gives us a script, we need to ask and figure it out with our partner as we go! And that means talking about it.

Beyond movies and TV, advertisements can have a big effect on the way we view sex and sexuality too. We see so many ads every day! Ads are constantly using sex to sell products to us. They imply that sex and attraction are something you can "buy" or "earn," like a reward. This view can make consent seem less important than the "reward" of sex, leading us to see people as objects. Think of the many advertisements and posters of people posed perfectly with almost no clothing on, often with their faces or heads cropped out of the pictures so they're just bodies. And those bodies are just objects of desire—something to be attained, bought, or earned.

These messages can train our brains to see *each other* as objects and possessions, instead of humans with feelings, rights, and desires of our own. If we associate other people's bodies with purchasing, buying, and "having," then we treat sex as a conquest. As mentioned, this mind-set makes consent seem unimportant. This is a dangerous association, because consent *is* important, legally, ethically, and emotionally. Try to notice the next time you see an ad or commercial that makes it seem like a person's body is a "prize" or something to be "bought" or "won over"—a thing you can acquire along with the product being sold.

Remember that plotlines aren't real life, and that movies and media aren't always the best examples of true and healthy consent.

Myth: Sex in Real Life Is Like Sex in Pornography

Things can also get complicated when it comes to pornography. Porn is more easily accessible and readily used now than in any other point in history, thanks to the internet. Pornography can in some ways satisfy curiosity and provide sexual experiences for people who use it in a healthy way, with education and understanding. Some people may use it to discover more about themselves, their bodies, and their sexuality. Masturbation is very healthy, and pornography is sometimes a tool people use during this activity. Partners may also choose to use porn consensually within their relationships as a tool for pleasure.

On the other hand, if we don't know how to interpret what we're looking at, porn can leave us with misleading expectations about how sex happens in real life.

Watching porn is a very personal decision that you may want to take some time to consider. Personal or family values might influence your decision. Some countries also have laws requiring you to be a certain age before watching pornography. Such laws are there to help keep you safe. Porn can put a whole lot of power in your hands without a lot of preparation. It can be like driving on the highway before you even have a learner's permit. Of course, you shouldn't feel guilty or shameful for being curious. It's normal and natural to be curious about these things. But let's take a moment to understand what porn is—and what it isn't—so that we don't misunderstand what we might see.

Ultimately, porn's purpose is to stimulate the viewer. It's not *really* made for the pleasure of the people involved in the scenes. It isn't meant to be educational, though people may view porn in this way if there isn't anyone around whom they feel comfortable asking about sexual intimacy. Porn shows a heightened reality for a specific purpose—for the pleasure of the viewer.

A lot of stuff goes on behind the scenes that you don't see: Actors are "fluffed" (prepared for scenes through ongoing masturbation or other stimulation off-set). Body parts are cleaned in various ways off-screen before filming. And positions, rhythms, progression of sexual acts, and "vocals" are planned for the visual or auditory stimulation of the viewer too.

Also, just like movies, porn scripts are written and reviewed off-screen before the actors even begin filming. Each person knows what is going to happen, even if the actors make it seem like they don't know or don't consent in the film itself. Since consent is given off-screen, porn typically doesn't include these moments of asking for or receiving consent during the actual film. But we need to know how to include consent in our *own* scripts in our *own* lives, even if it isn't what we might see in movies, TV, or pornography.

What this means is that porn doesn't work well as a model for real-life sexual intimacy. You can run into real danger if you use it as a model of what to do in real life—especially when the plotline involves doing things to another person that they didn't consent to. This is important.

Several young people in high school, college, and university have come through my office confused about sexual acts that they saw in pornography that didn't turn out well in real life. One young woman told me about something her male partner had done in their first sexual encounter. He'd seen actors slapping various body parts in porn, so he thought it was a normal thing to do during sex, and he didn't ask if she'd be okay with it.

You shouldn't assume something is okay without talking about it with your partner. And you shouldn't feel pressured to do something your partner hasn't asked about. Many people don't actually enjoy some of the sex acts you see in porn, which is why things need to be discussed specifically with your partners—*especially* anything involving aggression or force. You can't assume it's okay to engage in more aggressive sexual acts without checking with your partner first—and you shouldn't have to engage in those acts if someone else wants to and you don't, either. Remember, people need to be in control of the who, what, when, where, and *how* of sexual intimacy. Everyone has different preferences—and we need to ask each other to find out what each person consents to, and check in with each other as it's happening to make sure it's still enjoyable to everyone involved as things go.

Porn can be part of a healthy and fulfilling sex life if it aligns with your own morals, values, and choices—and your consent—and if you engage with it responsibly. If you choose to use porn, be conscious of the nature of what you're watching and remember to separate what may *seem* normal or common on-screen from what's *actually* normal and healthy in real life. Asking for consent is normal. Having informed consent with words and body language from all partners is normal. Checking in with partners before and during sex is normal. Mutual enjoyment in a sexual interaction is normal. Laughing, talking, and imperfect moments where things bump and make noises and maybe take a few tries to figure out is normal. Taking a break or pausing during a sexual activity and talking is normal. Having fun and being imperfect is normal—this is what intimacy is really about. It's about letting yourself be intimate and vulnerable with another person—which takes respect, trust, communication, and consent.

And know that, like everything else around sex and sexuality, watching pornography requires your consent as well. No one should show you anything or make you watch something that you haven't consented to watching. Some people may choose to use porn within their relationships, and some people may not. You're entitled to make that decision for yourself.

Myth: If You Do (This), That Means You Want Sex

Unfortunately, people are still judged today for their sexual choices. People who are considered very sexually active are often judged and insulted for it. Often you'll hear terms like "loose" or "slut" or "manwhore" used as insults against someone. These imply that someone's sexual choices make them "less than" or "bad." When certain people are viewed in this way, their consent can come to seem less important to those who don't understand consent.

This view makes it seem like it's okay for some people to be treated as objects. This can lead to a belief that it's *okay* to take advantage of that person—that somehow, if someone is sexually active, then whatever happens to them, even when it's hurtful, was somehow something they were "asking for." Or that what happens to them doesn't matter because they're already sexually active. But this isn't okay, or true. Everyone has the right to make their own sexual choices. And no one is ever entitled to anything when it comes to sex. No one is "asking for" anything other than what *they* freely consent to, themselves.

Let's take a quick moment to outline a few things that *don't* indicate consent beyond these activities themselves:

1. The clothing a person wears

2. Having drinks or being at a party

3. Friendly touching or hugging

4. Flirting with someone

5. Smiling or laughing at a joke

6. Accepting a drink from someone or allowing a person to pay for a dinner or movie

7. Accepting a walk home or a drive home

8. Being sexually intimate with other people

9. Being a single person, not in a relationship

10. Dancing or moving one's body in a sensual or sexy way

11. Being alone in a room with a person or going to someone's house alone

12. Staying out late or staying over at someone's house

13. Being open or talking openly about sex/sexuality or fantasies

14. Giving or receiving a compliment

15. Dancing with a person

16. Buying or accepting a gift from someone

17. Liking someone or having a crush on someone

18. Walking somewhere alone at any time of the day or night

It's true that some of these things *may* indicate possible interest from someone. But they also may not. The only way to know for sure is to *ask*—to talk about it. Most importantly, doing anything further requires explicit, talked-about consent.

Myth: Everyone Is Doing It

A lot of the time, it can feel like everybody but you is having sex or being sexually intimate. The statistics on this keep evolving, but right now they show that the majority of people are actually not having sexual intercourse until they're over the age of eighteen. In fact, almost 60 percent are waiting until they're older (Abma and

Martinez 2017). So, what we *think* people are doing and what's *actually* happening are often different. In any case, the most important thing to consider in your decision about what you choose to do is what's right for *you* and a consenting partner. Let yourself be free of any expectations of what you may *think* everyone else is doing.

If you think everyone is doing something, you may feel pressured to do that thing yourself, even if you don't actually want to. For example, it can sometimes feel expected that you should send your partners intimate pictures of yourself, often called "nudes." Or it can feel like you're obligated to receive them—even when you didn't ask for them. Just remember, consent applies here, too, as it does with any form of intimacy. You shouldn't have to send photos if you don't want to, and you shouldn't have to see others' photos if you don't want to.

While we're on this topic, another point to remember is that you never know where your photos might end up. Pictures last forever these days. And unfortunately, they can be used in ways we didn't intend. You shouldn't feel guilty about being curious about nudes or sexting. But do be cautious and think carefully about what you want and what's safe and healthy for you, including the safety of having nude photos on your phone or computer. (It's also true that, if you're under a certain age, there can be legal issues with nudes as well— some laws categorize them as child pornography if the person in the picture is under a certain age.) Your safety is always a priority. Know that your consent is important with nudes—even if it seems like "everyone is doing it." Remember that you're always entitled to your own choices and decisions, no matter what.

Myth: If You Don't Do What "Everyone" Is Doing, You're Not Cool

Just because something's common doesn't mean it's okay. That applies to how our society often treats sex and consent too. Hearing consent talked about as a joke or a meme, or the way it can be discussed in common conversation, can make things seem normal that aren't actually healthy.

For example, I remember the boys in middle school often talking about "copping a feel"—grazing a girl's butt or breast without her knowing or expecting it. This phrase was used so often and sounded so casual that I think most of us thought it was just normal. But in fact, it's not okay—even though it was made to sound and seem like it was normal. Touching someone without their permission is wrong.

We have to be aware of the concepts we're exposed to most often. Let's explore a few more of the common examples of messages or beliefs in our society that might seem "normal" but actually aren't:

- **You have to, those are the rules.** This message appears in games like spin the bottle, truth or dare, or seven minutes in heaven, whose rules say that you can't refuse to do something sexual if you're chosen in the game—without regard for consent or whether you actually want to do something. While you can play these games to explore sexuality, do know that even if you agree to play a game, you can also stop at any point. Make sure you're checking in with how you really feel at any moment. And if something really doesn't feel okay for you—no matter what *anyone else* says or what the "rules" of a game happen to be—you can *always* say no or leave a situation if you aren't comfortable. And remember anyone else in the game has that right too.

- **You have to agree if someone "cooler" than you wants something sexual, because you're so lucky.** If someone more popular than you asks you to do something sexual, it can seem like you have to do that thing—it would be a social disaster if you turned them down! Everyone wishes they could be with "that person." You would be crazy if you didn't want to do something with them! Not true. No matter how cool or desirable someone else is in the eyes of others, or even in your own eyes, if you aren't ready to do something sexual with someone, that person should respect your wish. Someone who truly wants to be with you for who you are, not just for what you can provide them, will respect your choice, no matter how popular they seem to be. If they don't, maybe they weren't really that cool to begin with.

  And if your friends don't think you're cool because you turned someone down who they thought was really desirable, or if they only want to hang out with you because of who you've been sexually intimate with, then those friendships likely aren't very deep or respectful either. True friends should value your decisions and encourage you to do what's right and best for you, no matter who is asking you out or wanting to be intimate with you.

- **It's not cool to say no.** It's not unusual to think that "all the popular kids are doing it" (being sexually intimate), or that it can make you lame or a prude or unpopular if you don't have sex. Sex is often portrayed as cool and exciting (like in movies, TV, and ads). And sex *can be* cool and exciting. But it's also a big step emotionally. You should think about it carefully, and make sure you feel ready for any intimacy based on your own reasons, morals, and values—not because of a fear that others won't think you're cool if you don't do something sexual.

Remember that if people only think you're cool if you do certain sexual things, those probably aren't the people you want to be friends with anyway. Those people don't sound like they respect you, your rights, and your ability to make your own decisions. While it can be hard to go against the grain or turn down someone who's "popular," remember that what makes you cool is being strong and true to yourself, and the right people in your life will see this and respect this.

- **Someone will like me more if I...** Society and the media can often make it seem like *only* people who are "sexy" or who do sexy things are valuable or likable, which isn't true. Everyone has value, no matter their sexual choices. But because of this message, it's easy to feel like someone we're interested in will like us more if we're sexually intimate with them. This assumption isn't correct—at least, not in a way that's healthy, respectful, or meaningful. Someone who likes you more for doing something sexual with them, even when you aren't ready to do it yourself, isn't someone who truly likes you or respects you. It's an unhealthy kind of relationship, because that person cares more about what you can do for them than about your comfort and safety.

It's not okay if someone makes you feel like you *have* to do something with them, without listening or respecting your feelings. Your safety and comfort should always come first in any healthy relationship. And you never need to use your body to make someone like you. You are already likable and lovable, and the right person will see this and respect your decisions.

- **If you loved me, then you would...** Because sex or intimacy can be a sign of affection, some people believe that if you like someone, you have to do sexual things with them to "show" or "prove" that love. But you don't have to if you don't want to! There are lots of ways to show you care for someone even if you aren't ready to be physically intimate with them. You can spend time together, buy or make small gifts for each other, share laughs, and share stories. You can be each other's confidants and safe spaces to talk about dreams and fears, likes and dislikes. If anyone ever tries to tell you "If you loved/liked me you would have sex with me" (or something along those lines), know that no person who loves or likes you should ever try to convince you to do something you aren't comfortable with doing. A person who likes or loves you will respect your comfort levels, your decisions, and your right to your own body. If you find yourself in this situation, you might respond with something like, "If you loved/liked me, you wouldn't ask me to do something that I'm not comfortable with."

- **You created this problem, now you have to fix it.** Sometimes, when someone is aroused by another person, they think that person is responsible for "fixing" their arousal through orgasm. You may have heard the phrase "blue balls"—it implies someone is leaving the person who's complaining of discomfort hanging if they don't do whatever sexual action the complainer has in mind. It implies the other person has a responsibility to continue a sexual act, even if they don't want to. This is simply not true. No one is ever responsible for anyone else's arousal—it doesn't matter if someone is turned on or not. If the other person doesn't want to do anything further sexually, it should stop there, immediately. Each person has the power to take care of their own arousal. And no one ever has a responsibility to do anything they aren't comfortable with, no matter what "reason" someone else might give.

Myth: Just Say No

As we discussed in the introduction to this book, if someone says no, it *definitely* **means no**! But we should include "just say no" here as a myth because of the implications that this message can have for the way we practice consent. It's still missing something.

For one thing, this message puts a lot of responsibility on the other person to say no. Let's think about that. If all we're expecting is that anything goes *until* a partner says no, then we aren't looking for consent to proceed—we're looking for self-defense to *stop* proceeding. But consent means understanding that it's not "green light until a red light appears"; it's about asking permission from our partners to move forward, assuming it's a red light until we're told otherwise.

If you're initiating sexual intimacy, it's up to *you* to make sure you ask for your partner's consent for whatever it is you hope to do. It isn't just the other person's responsibility to say no. What's more, the "just say no" message assumes that the person being approached is in a state of mind where they can *say* no. And this is an assumption that isn't always correct (we will explore this more in chapter 3).

So we know that consent isn't just a "no"—and what's more, it isn't always just a "yes," either. There are lots of things to consider when we look at the idea of consent. Things like these: What types of relationships are appropriate to look for consent from in the first place? And what state of mind do people need to be in to be able to give consent? There are lots of things that come together to create total consent. Let's dive in deeper now to look at all the nuances of what consent *really* looks like.

CHAPTER 2

What Is Consent?

Now that we know a bit more about ourselves and a lot of the things that *aren't* consent, let's take a deeper dive into the nuances of what *is* consent. We know that it's not just a simple question, with a yes or no answer. We know it's a total picture of the who, what, when, where, why, and how of a sexual situation. There are lots of other pieces to it that are very important to know too.

One of the best places to get grounded in some of the nuances of consent is the law. The laws around consent can provide an outline of what is and *isn't* okay when we start thinking about consent and sexual activity. The law helps us understand some of the important building blocks of the finer points of what true consent looks like.

Once we explore how the law can help us get the full picture of consent, we'll then look at the other aspects of consent that are super important in making sure it's total. These other aspects of consent—honest communication, ongoing communication, and more you'll learn about in this chapter—make up the acronym HOT SPICE. We'll talk about what each of these letters stands for and how they can help us understand all the different pieces of consent.

So let's start putting these pieces together—starting with the law.

CONSENT AND THE LAW

Each country, state, and province may define their laws slightly differently, so you may want to look up the more specific details for the area in which you live. But the overarching ideas are generally similar, which we'll explore here in broad terms.

There are several things you have to take into account before a sexual interaction should be considered.

The first is *capacity to consent*. This has to do with whether someone is able to give consent to a sexual encounter in the first place. Is it a safe or fair thing for a given set of people to even be *considering* being sexually intimate with each other?

There are a few factors to consider to make sure no one's being taken advantage of or put into an unsafe situation. The things that can make someone unable to give safe (and legal) consent are:

1. **Age.** Legally, children and anyone who's under legal age— which varies, but is often around sixteen to eighteen years old—can't give consent to sexual acts with adults. These laws help people from being taken advantage of or exposed too early to things they're not developmentally ready for. Even if someone under the legal age seems to be giving verbal consent, this still isn't considered legal consent. It's the adult's responsibility to know the laws and know it isn't appropriate to ask someone underage in the first place.

Laws often make exceptions for people who are under the age of consent but close in age to each other. The main intent of these laws is to ensure that *older* people aren't taking advantage of younger people, while leaving space for younger people to explore their sexuality with their peers safely. For instance, a country or state may outline that a fourteen-year-old can consent with someone who is less than five years older than they are. In another place, it might be legal for a twelve-year-old to be sexually intimate with someone two years older. In the end, the exact laws depend on where you live. Be sure you know the laws in your particular area; it'll be a starting point for consent that we'll build on in the rest of this book.

2. **Power relationships.** *Power* in this context is the ability to control another person in some way. When someone is in a position of power over another person—like a teacher with a student, or a doctor with a patient, or a coach with a basketball player—they can't ethically engage in a sexual relationship with the person they have power over. The difference in power between the two people removes the less powerful person's ability to give true consent. The less powerful person may not feel that they can safely say what they really want or don't want. They may feel like they *have* to do something if asked, or that they can't truly say no without consequences. We're often taught to listen to authority figures no matter what, so these types of power relationships don't make for safe sexual relationships with true and freely given consent.

3. **Family relationships.** It's also illegal for family members to have sexual relationships. These laws ensure that children aren't being taken advantage of in their homes and safe spaces where they're often most vulnerable.

4. **Conscious capacity.** If someone is unconscious or under the influence of drugs or alcohol, they can't give consent to a sexual act. They aren't "there"—mentally present and aware—as their full, normal self to be able to give consent. Consent has to come from a wholly aware person—not a drugged or incapacitated version of a person.

   What does it mean to be *intoxicated*? Well, it depends. There are different legal definitions in different areas. But in general, someone who's *not* intoxicated is in full control of their mental abilities. Being sober allows us to make informed and rational choices from a clear mind, which makes a safe and fair interaction possible. If you aren't sure about a potential partner's intoxication level, or you aren't sure of your own intoxication level, think about proceeding much more carefully, or perhaps not at all. Any degree of intoxication can impair a person's ability to communicate their true consent. (There is more to this discussion, so we'll talk more about drugs and alcohol in chapter 5.)

5. **Ability to consent.** Someone with a physical or developmental disability, incapacity, or other form of vulnerability may not be able to freely give affirmative consent to a sexual act. This aspect of capacity to consent, like the others,

keeps people from being taken advantage of. With this rule as with the others, each person's particular situation may be different. But ability is something we want to be thinking about in terms of safety for everyone involved.

So, the first question is always: Do you and a potential partner each have the legal capacity to consent when you consider the above points? If the answer is yes—on all counts—then we look at the next two elements of consent. These have to do with the actual *expression* of consent—how it's given:

- Is consent *freely given*? Has everyone offered consent of their own free will, without being forced or threatened, "talked into" something, or made to feel like they can't safely say no?

- Is consent *affirmative*? Has everyone expressed overt agreement, through actions and/or words, to sexual acts? Consent isn't just the absence of "no"—there needs to be a "yes," ideally with both words and body language, together.

All sexually intimate partners need to have full capacity to consent, and their consent needs to be both freely given and affirmative. That's our basic legal starting place for consent.

If you're initiating sexual activity, it's your responsibility to know how your partners are receiving your behavior. The following aren't valid excuses for someone initiating sex to skip getting consent:

- If the initiating partner is intoxicated

- If someone is reckless about whether the other person was truly consenting

- If someone didn't take proper steps to see if there was consent

- If someone chose to ignore signs that there was a lack of consent

None of these are reasons not to get consent! Each of us holds a legal (and moral) responsibility to understand and practice true consent. So let's keep learning!

TOTAL CONSENT: HOT SPICE

We're going to look at consent from a broader angle now, so that we make sure we're truly respecting everyone's capacity to consent, including our own. Once we've determined that a person has the appropriate *capacity to consent*, and that *affirmative consent* has been *freely given*, we then have a few more nuances to understand to make sure true consent is present.

For this, we need to add a little *HOT SPICE* to the mix—the eight main things we need to make sure are present for true consent. Let's have a look at what HOT SPICE stands for:

Honest

Ongoing

Talked-about

Specific

Present-moment

Informed

Changeable

Enthusiastic

Let's expand on each of these to see what they're all about.

Honest (Each Person Has Independently Checked in with Their True Feelings)

In a sexual encounter, each person should look at their own honest feelings in that moment about what they want and don't want. Sometimes, we can feel pressure to make someone else happy or not hurt their feelings, even when it comes to sexual activity. This can cause us to not be true to ourselves if we don't take the time to notice how *we* feel about something, outside of another person's wants or desires.

We each need to check in with our honest feelings about doing something sexual or intimate—how do we *really* feel about something? Have we separated what we really want from any external pressures? Only once we feel truly into an activity *ourselves* should we look at the idea of engaging in it with a partner. This is where true and total consent comes from—our own hearts and minds, first. This is an ideal first step. If you have the opportunity to create space for an honest check-in for yourself and your partner, it can help keep everyone safe.

Ongoing (We Ask and Look for Consent, Every Step of the Way)

Consent isn't a single moment or interaction—it's actually ongoing *throughout* an interaction. This means that any time someone *escalates* a sexual activity—any time they try something new, or take things a step further—they need to have their partner's consent for what they'd like to do. You should be on the same page with your partner at every stage. This means going slowly, getting and giving verbal (spoken) consent, and paying attention to body language. Notice what you and your partner are feeling, saying, and doing, to make sure everyone's still on the same page and into what's going on. Check in with your partner in some way as you go. Consent is an ongoing process and conversation throughout any interaction. (We'll talk about different ways to do this in chapter 3.)

Talked-About (Don't Rely Only on Body Language— Use Words and Body Language Together)

Sometimes we think we can read another person's nonverbal signals really well. And then we think we know what they want us to do or not do with them. But unfortunately, none of us is actually a mind reader, and this is a fairly unreliable strategy in real life. Body language is unreliable on its own, and a look or a gesture can be interpreted in a lot of ways. How do you know if someone looking at you in a particular way means they'd like a hug, a kiss, or more? What kind of look is "enough" to indicate someone's interested in sex? If you're struggling to answer these questions, it's because we can't tell these things based on body language alone. We have to *talk* about what's going on too.

Body language is even less reliable because we often tend to look for signs that confirm what we'd like to believe. So if we're interested in someone, we're more likely to interpret their behavior to mean the other person is interested in us too. When we're busy looking for the signs we *want* to see, we can miss other important body language signals. This is called *confirmation bias*. We can interpret a smile a hundred different ways (friendly, flirty, and so on), but we're more likely to see something that supports our hopes and beliefs. This makes our ability to interpret body language on its own even less reliable—which is another reason we have to *talk* about what's going on.

There is *no* reason not to talk about it before doing something sexual with a partner. Fear of rejection is not a reason to not talk about it. And fear of someone getting mad isn't a reason to not talk about it either. Don't guess what someone else is feeling. Be sure! Ask, and express what you're feeling. We need *both* verbal and body language to safely engage with a partner. (We'll dive deeper into just what this looks like in chapter 3.)

Specific (Consent for the Who, What, When, Where, Why, and How of Each Activity)

Each person also has the right to give or not give consent regarding:

- What they're doing—what the activity is

- Whom they're doing it with

- When they're doing it

- Where they're doing it

- How they're doing it

- Why they're choosing to do it

You and your partners need to give and get consent for each specific aspect of a sexual interaction. And consent to one activity doesn't mean consent to anything other than that. This is true both in terms of *what's* happening—consent to kissing, for instance, doesn't mean consent to sexual intercourse—and *how* it's happening: for example, consent to sexual intercourse isn't the same as consent to rough or aggressive sexual intercourse. Finally, specific consent needs to be obtained through verbal communication *and* body language.

Present-Moment (Only Consent at the Time of an Activity Is Consent)

Nothing other than affirmative, enthusiastic consent in the moment of each sexual encounter can be taken as consent. And there are no "free passes" on consent. You have to get it and give it *each time* you are intimate with another person. For instance, having been physically intimate with someone in the past isn't consent to future sexual encounters with that person. A person who's had sex with someone previously isn't required to have sex with them again. And an agreement to sex earlier in the day or at any other point in time isn't considered consent for the activity in the moment. Consent has to be reestablished in the moment itself. Finally, no one else can consent to something but the person themself. Only the person directly involved can consent in the present moment.

Informed (Having All the Necessary Details)

Each person engaging in sexual intimacy has the right to be fully informed about what they're consenting to, and with whom. This means that you and your partners are all truthful about:

- Your identity (who you are and your age)

- How sexual intimacy will take place (for example, consent to sex doesn't mean consent to a video being taken during sex)

- Your relationship status (this means consent to having sex with someone who's lied about being single isn't true consent)

- Which contraceptives you'll use, and how (agreeing to sex with a condom isn't consent to having sex without a condom)

- Any risks that your partners might need to be aware of, like the risk of sexually transmitted infections (STIs). Consenting to sex with someone without the knowledge that they're positive for an STI isn't true informed consent. (We'll talk more about STIs in chapter 5.)

Changeable (Anyone Can Withdraw Consent at Any Time)

Consent can be withdrawn *at any time* during a sexual interaction. You and your partners can change your minds, say no, or ask to stop an activity at any moment for *any* reason. Even in the middle of something, even if someone agreed to something earlier on in the day or earlier in the interaction—everyone has the right to withdraw consent at any time leading up to and during a sexual interaction. And if this happens, partners must listen and stop the activity at once.

A clear verbal statement, like "I'd like to stop," can be given at any time. But hesitating, slowing down, or not responding in an enthusiastic way any longer can also be signs that consent isn't present. If this happens, we need to stop whatever we're doing, and connect with and communicate with our partner about what they might be feeling or thinking.

Enthusiastic (Each Person Is Fully Present and Fully "Into It")

Enthusiastic means that everyone is on the same page and into what's going on. It means that each person is *choosing* to be there, and they're glad, excited, or enthusiastic about what's happening. No one should be passively lying there or robotically going through the motions. No one should be emotionally or mentally absent. If someone seems robotic or passive, they might not be okay with what's happening (we'll explore this more in chapter 3). This is why we're looking for enthusiastic consent. We want to make sure that everyone feels safe in a moment of sexual intimacy, and that everyone's emotionally and mentally present. Enthusiastic consent doesn't mean having the best sex of your life (and bad sex—which could encompass feeling awkward during intimacy, you or a partner not reaching climax, or not feeling the right chemistry with a partner—doesn't mean consent isn't present, which we'll talk more about in chapter 6). What it means is that you and each of your partners are emotionally present and feeling safe and engaged in whatever intimacy you're sharing.

And all of this can only happen when we have all the basics of consent. Remember: each person should be fully conscious and in control of their actions, should have the capacity to consent due to age and developmental and physical ability, and shouldn't be intoxicated. No person should be vulnerable in the situation or acting recklessly, and there should be no unsafe power dynamics. If at any point someone's enthusiasm goes away, and any hesitation or reservation in voice or body language appears, the activity needs to stop, and the partners should check in with each other about what they're thinking and feeling.

When you put together what the law teaches us about consent with what we learned from HOT SPICE, we can see the foundation of total consent. Again, total consent is when sexual partners are in control of:

- What they choose to do

- With whom

- When and where they choose to do it

- How they choose to do it

- Why they choose to do it

Understanding consent is vital and important for safe, healthy, and enjoyable intimacy. So it's important to understand what it looks like and what it sounds like when consent is present, and when it's not—that is, how to communicate consent. That's what we'll explore next.

CHAPTER 3

Communicating with Consent

In this chapter, we'll look at the concrete ins-and-outs of consent: what it looks like to ask, and what it looks like when consent is given and when it's not. We're going to look at giving and receiving signals and signs. Then we're going to dive a little deeper to understand the nuances of *why* it's so important to notice nonverbal signs like hesitating, shutting down, or going quiet. We'll look at the mechanisms of the *survival response* in our brains and bodies: the ways our bodies and brains respond when we're faced with something that feels scary or threatening. This will help us understand how we both ask for and give consent to our partners—and how to notice if something doesn't look or feel right. Nuances can be hard to pick up on—and this will help you become much more consent-literate.

This chapter's discussion of communication is designed to help you pay attention to your partner, check in with them, and notice if they seem comfortable or not, even if they haven't directly told you. In chapter 4, we'll look at ways you can communicate with your partner if you're feeling uncomfortable yourself.

WHAT CONSENT LOOKS AND SOUNDS LIKE

Communication generally has two main parts—our *verbal consent*, which is our words (sometimes also called *explicit consent*), and our *nonverbal* or *body language consent* (sometimes also called *non-explicit* or *implied consent*). To be more specific:

- *Verbal consent* is when you make it clear using your words what you want or don't want.

- *Nonverbal* or *body language consent* is when you use body language and other nonverbal means to communicate your consent and desire.

So what exactly does this all look like and sound like?

Clear Communication: Your Go-To Guide

This section is your go-to list of things to look for, in terms of both verbal and nonverbal consent.

Remember that you should have *both* verbal consent *as well as* nonverbal consent. Together, these give us affirmative, enthusiastic consent. We want words and body language to match.

The lists below can give you a good idea of the types of things to look for. But they don't include everything. If you aren't sure what signals your partner is giving, or how to interpret what your partner is doing, *ask!*

Ways to Ask

As we've explored, we don't have a script in real life, so sometimes it can feel like we have to make it all up ourselves. The good news is, it isn't as hard as it seems! Asking for consent in real life can be cool, sexy, intimate, and totally natural. There are a couple ways you can approach it. Here are some ideas.

1. **Ask directly.** This might sound something like this: "Would it be okay if I…?" or "May I (do something)?" or "Are you interested in (something with me)?"

2. **Make a suggestion—and check in with your partner.** You might say, "I would really like to (do something); are you into that too?" or "This is hot. I'd love to make you feel even better, and (suggest how you'd like to do that). Would you like that?" Or, more casually, "I keep thinking about kissing you. Do you think about it too?"—and if the answer is yes, then follow up with a direct "Do you want to?"

3. **Ask your partner for their direction.** You might ask what your partner wants to do, or wants you to do. "What do you want me to do next?" or "What would you like us to try?"

4. **Check for comfort and consent as things go.** "Does this feel okay for you?" might be a good question to ask, or "Is this all right?"

   Pro-tip: Encourage communicating about consent from each other as you go! Sometimes we can feel like we're not comfortable or confident expressing what we want or don't want to a partner, for fear of disappointing them. You can make this easier by being upfront about the fact that you *want* them to be honest with you about what they want. You might say something like this: "I'm really excited to be with you, but I want you to know that your comfort is the most important thing to me. If at any point you need me to stop or slow down, I want you to tell me, and that's totally cool—I want us both to feel safe and comfortable, no matter what."

Also, you can ask for a bit of direction from your partner on what consent looks like for them: "I want you to feel totally comfortable as we do this. Is there anything I should know ahead of time that's a sign you're not okay? Or is there anything you know you're not comfortable with or don't want me to do?"

Once we have asked for consent from a partner, what does it look like to have enthusiastic, affirmative consent? Let's look at some of the possible "yes" signals.

"Yes!"—Proceed (With Ongoing Consent as You Go)

Signs of **Verbal** *Consent ("Yes!")*

Remember, these words are not enough for enthusiastic, affirmative consent on their own. Rather, the idea is that these are the kinds of words that *line up with* nonverbal consent (which we'll look at in the next section), to signal that what's happening is something a person wants.

- 👍 "Yes!"
- 👍 "I want to do this!"
- 👍 "I want that!"
- 👍 "Sure!"
- 👍 "I'm ready!"
- 👍 "Don't stop!"
- 👍 "I love this!"
- 👍 "Can you (the person makes a suggestion to their partner here)?"
- 👍 "I'd like that."
- 👍 "Yes, a little bit more."
- 👍 "I'm so glad you asked me."
- 👍 "I'm so into this/you."
- 👍 "I've wanted to do this for so long."
- 👍 "This is amazing/so hot!"
- 👍 "I'd love to!"

Signs of **Nonverbal** *Consent (Body Language That Signals
"I'm Into This!")*

Again, these are not enough for enthusiastic, affirmative consent on their own. These are body language signals that *line up with* verbal consent (see previous section), to signal that what's happening is something a person wants.

- 👍 Nodding yes
- 👍 Smiling or laughing
- 👍 Shoulders turned toward you
- 👍 Leaning in close or pressing against you
- 👍 Eye contact and smiling
- 👍 Pulling you closer
- 👍 Making enthusiastic noises
- 👍 Moaning or sighing
- 👍 Moving with you/against you
- 👍 Confidently returning a kiss or a certain motion; confidently reciprocating a certain activity
- 👍 Grabbing or stroking you with their hands
- 👍 Nuzzling or cuddling against you

These are some examples of what an affirmative enthusiastic "yes" might look like—a yes in which a person's verbal consent (their words) matches their nonverbal consent (their body language).

Now, what might it look like if someone *isn't* giving you their consent for something?

"No"—Stop Whatever You're Doing and Check In

Signs of **Verbal** *Non-Consent ("No")*

- "No, I'm not interested."

- "I don't want to do this."

- "I don't want that."

- "Stop."

- "I don't know."

- "I don't like this."

- "This feels wrong."

- "I thought I wanted this, but..."

- "I want to do this, but not right now."

- "Umm.../Oh..."

- Nervous giggling instead of answering directly

- Changing the subject or dodging the question

- "I have a boyfriend/girlfriend/partner..."

- "I just want to hang out with my friends tonight."

- "Can we slow down?"

- "Whoa/Hey/Listen..."

- "Where did everyone else go?"

- "Hey, what if we did (this) instead?" (said hesitantly)

- If a partner offers some other form of intimacy than what you asked for consent to do, this may also be a sign they're not comfortable with what you're asking, and they don't know how to let you know that. And it's a sign you need to stop what you're doing and check in with them more clearly.

*Signs of **Nonverbal** Non-Consent*

Nonverbal non-consent is body language that signals "This isn't okay, I'm uncomfortable, let's stop."

- 👎 Silence
- 👎 Freezing up
- 👎 Tensing up
- 👎 Shaking head
- 👎 Turning away/looking away
- 👎 Pushing away
- 👎 Holding breath/not breathing properly
- 👎 Crying/tears
- 👎 Avoiding eye contact
- 👎 If your partner was responding to you in an enthusiastic way, but suddenly stops responding
- 👎 If your partner shuts down: silence, blank facial expression, just lying there
- 👎 If your partner responds to you in a way that's not enthusiastic—for example, they kiss you back but no other signs of nonverbal consent are present. Maybe something feels "off" or robotic.

If a partner says no directly, changes the subject, or withdraws or shuts down, those are all signs of non-consent. Any sexual activity should stop immediately and you should check in with your partner to see what they're feeling and thinking.

Beyond "Just Say No"

Sometimes it can be a bit confusing to understand exactly why a partner can't just say the word "no" during sexual intimacy, an idea we began to explore back at the end of chapter 1. We say no easily in so many other areas of our lives—no to borrowing money, or no to someone asking to cut in line if we're in a rush. But sometimes it isn't as easy as it would seem to "just say no" when it comes to sexual intimacy.

Our brains and bodies are very complicated, and sexual intimacy is a vulnerable thing, involving some pretty vulnerable parts of our anatomy and our emotions. And so we can react to it in intensely physical ways—ways we may not respond in other, regular, everyday situations. It's much more intense—when someone asks for sexual consent from us, it makes us vulnerable. Which can affect how we react in that moment.

Our bodies and brains will always try to do their best to navigate any situation safely. In many cases, this means a lot of other responses may come to the surface first, instead of a strong, confident "yes" or "no." We'll take a moment here to understand why that is, and what it looks like.

A lot of different things can make saying no to a partner feel scary, which we'll explore throughout this section and in chapter 4. Things like physical size, social pressure, or how safe we feel in a physical space with someone can influence how safe it feels to say no in an unwanted or uncomfortable sexual situation. When we don't know how a partner might react, the idea of someone getting mad at or upset with us for saying no can feel scary—physically, socially, or emotionally. These fears can send signals to our bodies and brains to try to keep us safe.

And these reactions are sometimes a bit different than we'd expect. For this reason, we're going to get to know more about our brains and bodies in this next section.

UNDERSTANDING OUR REACTIONS

It's important to understand what goes on in our brains and our bodies so that we can interpret what we're seeing or experiencing during a sexual interaction—both in ourselves and in our partners. When we know the nuances of how our bodies react, we can be clearer about noticing these things and respecting the signs that we see in our partners and ourselves. So let's look at what's going on under the surface so we can better understand our and our partners' reactions during moments of consent.

To understand why we think and react the way that we do, we should first get briefly introduced to our permanent residence—our body.

Our brains have a system that works at all times to keep us safe, whether we're aware of it or not. Your body is doing all sorts of things right now to make sure you're alive and well—things you aren't telling it to consciously do. Right now, your body is keeping you at a regular temperature, digesting your food, and pumping blood to your organs and muscles. These are all things you aren't telling it to do with your thoughts—things that help keep you alive and safe. So it makes sense that your body does some things to keep you safe emotionally too— things that you aren't always consciously telling it to do.

There's a whole system inside you that's designed to help keep you safe. And this system comes into play in sexual interactions.

We're going to imagine a model to help illustrate this system. We'll call it the Survival House (see figure 1). This model will be particularly helpful in illustrating why, in a sexual situation, someone might not be able to respond in the way that we might expect. I hope after we explore this model, you'll be able to better understand how we communicate and react when it comes to sex and consent. You'll see a bunch of things in the house: a couch, stairs, telescopes, a ladder, and a slide. Don't worry; we'll explore what each of these stands for in the pages to come.

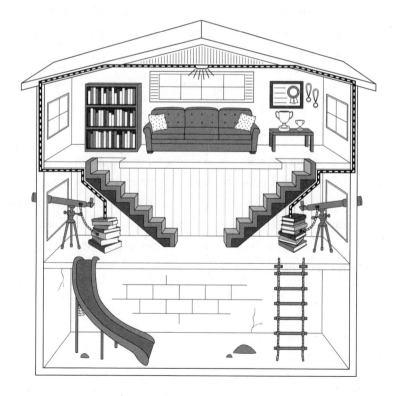

Figure 1: The Survival House

The Survival House

The Survival House is a house with three floors. Each floor represents a part of our brain and an area of our nervous system. These three floors are where our bodies process our level of comfort with a sexual interaction.

Here's a brief overview of what each floor represents:

- The top floor is our rational brain and the part of our nervous system that handles social situations.

- The middle floor is our emotional brain and the part of our nervous system that handles active defense and response.

- The bottom floor is our instinctive brain and the part of our nervous system that handles passive defense and response.

The Top Floor: "Green Light"

The top floor of the Survival House represents the most recently evolved, human part of our brains and nervous systems: the neocortex (the outside of the brain—see figure 2), and all the nerves in our head and face (this is known as the ventral vagal complex—see figure 3). Let's start there to understand our experience during intimacy and consent.

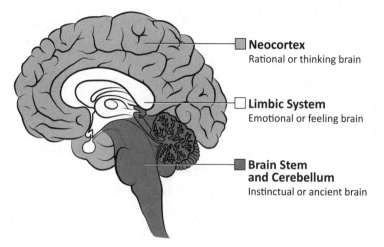

Figure 2: The Triune (Three-Layered) Brain (MacLean 1990)

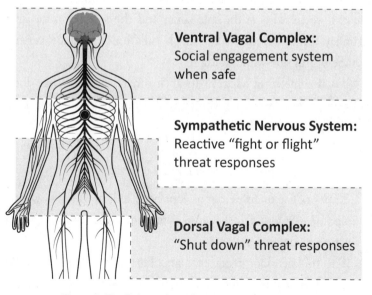

Figure 3: The Polyvagal and Sympathetic Nervous System
(Porges 2017)

The top floor is the floor that consensual sex should happen on—which is represented in the image as the couch, where intimacy happens. When we're on this floor, we're in the part of our brain that evolved most recently to handle the stuff that goes into being a social mammal, which is what humans are. When this social mammal brain is in control, it means we're feeling safe. And we have the ability to think rationally, use complex language, and clearly know and remember things. Our ability to do these things is represented in the diagram as the bookshelf on the top floor. This is where we store our knowledge, memories, language, and skills, like books on a shelf. When your body is "on the top floor" in a sexual moment with someone, you can think and speak clearly about what you want and don't want. You're able to make conscious, rational decisions. Your body feels safe, giving you a *green light* to go ahead, if you choose to. This is the safe zone, and the safe floor, for sexual intimacy. On this floor, we can laugh, talk, touch, and feel generally confident and safe while doing so.

But if something happens in an intimate moment that doesn't feel right, there's a chance you can fall from the top floor into the middle floor of the house.

The Middle Floor: "Yellow Light"

Think of the middle floor as your body telling you to slow down, giving you a *yellow light* because something doesn't feel safe, and activating its defense systems.

The middle floor represents an older part of your brain that developed when our evolutionary ancestors (like reptiles) lived much less social lives. This part of your brain contains the limbic system (see figure 2), which is the emotional part of the brain that's alert to things that might threaten us. This system controls the way we react when we don't feel completely safe.

The middle floor also represents the *sympathetic nervous system.* Have you heard of the *fight-or-flight response?* It's our body's response to stress, when our heart races, our breathing speeds up, and our stomach feels queasy as we prepare to either fight what we're facing or get away from it (flight). Together the limbic system and fight-or-flight nervous system generally make up the experience we have on the middle floor of the house.

If you're on the middle floor of the house in a sexual situation, a more instinctive, less rational part of your body is operating. Because of this, you might not be able to access your top-floor assertive responses—your ability to communicate a strong yes or a strong no. Instead, your body might use fight-or-flight responses. In a sexual interaction, *flight* responses can look like hesitating, laughing nervously, or trying to change the subject. *Fight* responses can look like trying to create physical distance or push away from the person.

Another middle-floor reaction our bodies have is the *freeze response.* Basically, when you're facing something that's scary for you, your emotions are running high. Your body may be doing moment-to-moment calculations to figure out what seems least risky—least likely to make the situation worse—and how you can get out of a situation quickly and safely. This can look and feel like "doing nothing" while your brain and body are super activated, trying to gather information on the safest next step to take. This is why watching for hesitation in yourself or a partner is so important. It can be a sign of a middle-floor yellow-light response.

Another middle-floor defensive reaction is *appeasement* (Bloom and Farragher 2010). This is important. Appeasing someone means doing something that you think will make them happy that you might not want to do yourself. For example, offering someone oral sex instead of intercourse.

A related middle-floor response is *tend and befriend* (Byrd-Craven, Auer, and Kennison 2015; Taylor et al. 2000). This is when you do things to take care of a person who's disrespected you or your boundaries in some way—often because you feel, whether it's conscious or not, that this will prevent further pain now and in the future, or that there will be consequences if you don't tend to the person or stay friends with them.

Avoiding social threats from an unsafe person was a very important part of human evolution. Throughout human history, people have needed other people in order to survive. When humans were hunter-gatherers, survival was hard, if not impossible, all on our own. So needing to be accepted by others became a necessity for our ancestors' survival in small groups. That need to be accepted in order to ensure our safety still influences our behavior today. Which is why one response to an unsafe person is to be nice to that person, to try to please or take care of them, so we can remain part of the social group. We don't want to be kicked out, because historically, that might've meant that we'd die on our own. It's important to understand this instinct so we can be aware of our own reactions and set boundaries for ourselves. (We'll talk more about boundaries in chapter 4.)

These reactions are often outside our conscious control. Remember, we're not operating on the top-floor, rational part of our brains. Our bookshelf of rational skills, like the ability to communicate in clear language, is harder to reach! So it can be harder to find those statements of explicit consent we talked about at the beginning of this chapter. If someone can't find their words, it could be a sign that they aren't feeling safe and okay. If that happens, we should definitely stop and check in with each other.

In general, whether your first response is to fight, take flight, freeze, appease, tend, or befriend, the systems in your brain and body are working to find ways to "fix" the situation you're in and reduce risk. Different people have different "fix-it" responses. These are all ways that our bodies and brains believe they can reduce the feeling of being unsafe in a way that doesn't seem to increase the danger. Because everyone's different, we have to be aware of many signals.

When someone is on this yellow-light floor, it's definitely time to slow down, stop, and check in. And if you ever find yourself on this floor, it's important to know that your feelings are normal, and there's nothing wrong with the reactions you might have. Your brain and body are just trying to keep you safe.

But once we're aware that our bodies use these instinctive responses, we can notice it happening, pay attention to our own and others' comfort levels, and work to access those top-floor rational skills again so we can be assertive and respectful of our own and others' rights and safety. That said: if whatever is making us uncomfortable continues—or gets worse, if we feel trapped (when flight isn't an option) or helpless (when we can't fight)—we can often fall one floor further down in our Survival House.

The Bottom Floor: "Red Light"

The bottom floor represents the part of the brain and body that's most ancient. Back then, the best strategy when an animal was facing a threat was to find some place to hide to outlast their opponent. This involves shutting down, conserving energy, and just trying to make it through the experience.

This bottom floor is the point at which a *red light* comes on. On this floor, our brain and body essentially shut down. We go into the most ancient parts of the brain (the brain stem and cerebellum; see figure 2) and the lowest parts of our nervous system (the dorsal vagal complex; see figure 3). We can become nonresponsive, *dissociated* (when you don't feel like yourself, or when you feel like you're outside of your own body), or robotic (going through the motions). All you're trying to do is make it through the experience. This shutdown or frozen feeling is called *tonic immobility* (Möller, Söndergaard, and Helström 2017). And it happens quickly too. That's why there's a slide in the bottom floor in the Survival House diagram: this represents just how quickly we can enter a shutdown state. (And the ladder in the bottom floor represents how hard it can be, by comparison, to come out of this state once we've fallen into it.)

This may sound pretty extreme. And it is. But it can happen when we're faced with something in an intimate situation that we're not ready for or that doesn't feel safe. Or when the people we're with aren't respecting our rights to stay in control of what's happening to us or around us.

Remember the top floor of the house is where we feel safe and in control. When we're on the bottom floor—in shutdown mode—we're very far away from the top. No intimacy should happen on the bottom floor.

So let's put it all together and see what it looks like (figure 4). This is your quick reference guide to all the ins and outs of the Survival House.

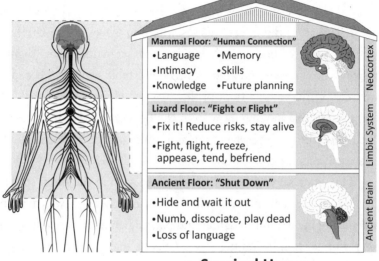

Mammal Floor: "Human Connection"
- Language
- Memory
- Intimacy
- Skills
- Knowledge
- Future planning

Neocortex

Lizard Floor: "Fight or Flight"
- Fix it! Reduce risks, stay alive
- Fight, flight, freeze, appease, tend, befriend

Limbic System

Ancient Floor: "Shut Down"
- Hide and wait it out
- Numb, dissociate, play dead
- Loss of language

Ancient Brain

Survival House

Figure 4: Survival House "Quick Reference" Diagram

Why This Matters

So why does all this matter? For one thing, the three floors of the Survival House—three responses to things we encounter in the world—help us understand why people sometimes aren't able to "just say no" in a sexual situation. A "no" response can often feel like an assertive response. And an assertive response doesn't always feel safe to us. If we feel intimidated or unsafe around someone, our instinct may be to not escalate things or anger that person. Sometimes, it feels safer to our bodies to appease them.

For instance, think about the story I told earlier in the book about when I was in school. When I went to all-ages dances with my friends, the boys we were with definitely went too far when they decided to dance against us without even asking if it was okay. What my friends and I did in response—switching places in the circle to get away from the boys who grabbed us—was a middle-floor "flight" response. My friends and I didn't feel comfortable saying no, because we were on the middle floor of the Survival House. And we didn't feel comfortable moving away from the boys without also trying to "befriend" them a bit by laughing and smiling. Both of these behaviors are also conflict-avoiding, defensive middle-floor responses.

This same set of responses can also be seen in the other stories I mentioned earlier in the book. Those times, while I was able to voice a no, my nervous laughter and playful behavior were efforts to keep things from becoming too serious or scary, and to maintain friendship feelings (the middle-floor appease and tend/befriend responses). They were yellow-light reactions, trying to deescalate a situation without causing more damage.

You can also think back to the story about my supervisor from work. Not only was he my supervisor—in a position of authority over me, and able to coerce or pressure me, meaning it was not an appropriate situation for consent (as we looked at in chapter 2)—but he also created a situation in which I felt physically trapped and helpless, and I wasn't able to do much but give in: the robotic, out-of-body bottom-floor response. This was a red-light response—an automatic reaction my body turned to in order to survive the experience. I was in a shutdown, survival mode. And though I was moving around, I wasn't really there. None of this was my fault; it was my body doing its best to survive the situation.

But when I got home at the end of the night and I was back in a place of relative safety, I moved up to the second floor of my Survival House. Then, all the emotions finally hit me. I panicked and cried—reactions from the emotional center of my brain. And then I threw up: a reaction linked to the stress systems controlled by the middle- and top-floor nervous systems.

If I had known about the Survival House back then, I would've understood that the reactions I had in those situations were normal. But I didn't know, so I was stuck feeling confused and scared—knowing that the things that were happening to me were wrong, but not knowing what I could do about them. And I was left feeling ashamed of myself afterward, as well as scared of similar situations happening again.

The other stories I told, about the student who offered oral sex instead of intercourse, and the student who felt pressured into having sex with someone who wasn't his girlfriend, also feature middle-floor, appeasement responses. Both of those students felt trapped and unsafe, and didn't want to escalate the situation.

With something as important as sexual intimacy, our bodies react in deep and emotional ways. We react before we even know what's happening to us. Our bodies and brains are always working to keep us safe.

And if we keep this in mind as we approach our partners, we can be intimate with others without feeling shame for how we might respond. We can understand all the nuances of communicating consent. And we can truly follow all the rules of total consent with the people we're sexually intimate with. Here's the thing: if we know more about what can cause us to fall from one floor of the Survival House to another, maybe we can intervene before any of us falls at all.

What Causes Yellow- and Red-Light Responses?

There are three main things that can send a person from the top floor of their Survival House to the middle or bottom floors: feeling helpless or trapped, the possibility of rejection, and past experiences. All of these things feel like they threaten our physical or emotional well-being.

Feeling helpless or trapped. When someone feels this way, they may feel like they have no choice but to go along with what's happening. It can be a feeling of being physically trapped—for instance, if you feel cornered in a room or pressed down by a body. Or it can be emotional, like if someone's coming on to you too strong, or if they make you feel like you can't say no or let them know you're uncomfortable with something.

Feeling helpless or trapped is the biggest trigger that can send you to the bottom floor of the house, shutting you down, because in these situations your middle-floor instincts for "fight" (being assertive) and "flight" (finding some way to get out of the situation) are blocked. And shutting down becomes what your body does to survive. If the middle-floor responses aren't working, the body drops you one more floor to try to survive what's happening.

This is why it's essential in intimate moments for everyone involved to feel safe in stating what they want or don't want. And why it's important that no one pressure anyone into doing something they don't want to do, either with their words or with their physical presence.

Rejection. Fear of rejection can also cause us to fall from the top floor of our Survival House to the middle or bottom floor. It's easy to be afraid that if we say no to someone, we'll be disliked, teased, made fun of, or bullied. As we discussed above, acceptance is important to us as humans—we are hardwired for human connection (Brown 2012). We evolved to need other people for survival.

So it can sometimes seem safer to appease or befriend someone (middle-floor responses) than to say no to them. We're afraid both that they'll reject us and that they'll feel rejected by us, causing them to lash out. But remember, the right people in your life—true friends and worthy partners—will respect your boundaries and decisions.

If you notice yourself wanting to appease someone so they won't be mad at you, remember that you are *absolutely allowed* to set boundaries and say no. Once you're aware of your body's natural responses to these situations, you can understand why your initial reaction might be to stay safe by appeasing, but then remind yourself of your right to say no, even if you feel nervous or upset. And if you don't feel safe saying no directly for any reason, excuse yourself to the bathroom or some other safe place and create some space to make a plan and call a friend, call a ride, or try to call someone for help. For a more in-depth discussion of unsafe situations, see chapter 6.

Past experiences. Our reactions in the present can be influenced by things that have happened to us in the past. This is especially true of intimate and vulnerable moments. Memories of times we've felt trapped, helpless, attacked, rejected, abandoned, or out of control are stored in a part of our fight-or-flight brain called the *amygdala*, which is part of the limbic system (the middle floor of the house). Like the other reactions we've discussed, storing painful memories is a defense mechanism our bodies developed to keep us safe. These memories are represented in the diagram by the stacks of books on the middle floor of the Survival House (figure 1).

These memories are unique to each of us. And sometimes, we're not even aware that our brains have stored up painful memories. But our subconscious minds remain on the lookout for situations that remind us of past danger and pain. We're extra sensitive to situations that remind us of our bookstack memories. This sensitivity is represented by the telescopes that are linked up to each bookstack in our emotional brain, in our subconscious. This process is called *neuroception*: when our bodies are on the lookout for threats from past memories, even if we aren't aware of it in our conscious brains (Porges 2017).

If the telescopes sense something that reminds us of a bookstack memory (a tone of voice, a fight or an argument, etc.), it can knock over the bookstack it's attached to. This sets our body's alarm system off, and we drop from the top floor of the house (safety and rational control) to the middle or bottom floor, where our defense systems take over.

Because all of us have our own past experiences and warning signals, one person might be sensitive to situations, words, or experiences that another person isn't sensitive to, and *that* person might be sensitive to a whole different set of experiences. What pulls one person down to the middle floor of the house—what makes them feel uncomfortable or unsafe—might be different than what sets off another person's defenses. No two people are alike, so we can't make assumptions about what feels safe for each person.

This is why it's so important to *observe* the signs and signals your partner is giving you *in the moment* without *assuming* how they might or should react. This is why it's so important to go slowly, especially with new partners, and to always be kind and respectful with them— and with yourself. And this is why it's so important to make sure that you *and* your partner both feel safe in every aspect of consent— the who, what, when, where, why, and how of what's happening.

This is also why the "E" of HOT SPICE is so important. Enthusiastic affirmative consent helps us make sure that our partners—and we ourselves—aren't dropped out-of-body and shut down in the bottom floor of the house. People should be moving and participating, vocalizing, and generally appearing to "be there" during intimacy.

So how can we boost feelings of safety and security with a partner? The better we communicate about consent, the more likely each partner is to stay on the top floor of the house, and the safer we feel. Let's have a look at some of the important pieces of that puzzle—boundaries, rejection, and healthy relationships.

CHAPTER 4

Applying the Skills

In the previous chapters, we discussed what consent is, the different responses we can have to sexual situations, and how to communicate with a partner about these things in a healthy way. Now let's look at two more crucial skills: establishing and setting boundaries, and dealing with rejection.

Now that we understand our bodies' defense mechanisms, we can work *with* these reactions in healthy ways to communicate about consent. When we think about things like boundaries and rejection ahead of time, and we know in advance what to do and what to expect, we can help ourselves and our partners by communicating clearly. So let's get started with these two very important concepts.

BOUNDARIES AND SAYING NO

Everyone has the right to say what's okay for them and what's not okay for them. This is called setting boundaries. Sometimes this involves saying no to something or turning someone down. As we explored in chapter 1, a lot of this begins on your own as you consider questions and decide what you feel ready for and with whom, and what you don't feel ready for. You're getting to know your own boundaries.

Sometimes it can be tough to think of the right way to say no to someone or to turn them down. Know that you can say no *however* you want to, even if it's just a simple "No," "No thanks," or "Sorry, I'm not interested." But sometimes you might want different words or ways to express yourself and your boundaries to someone.

If it feels safe to you, it's good to be respectful when communicating your boundaries and declining consent, especially with someone who has also been kind and respectful in how they've asked for your consent. Remember that it can be challenging for people to put themselves out there, so we want to be respectful in return with people's emotions when we're able to.

Think about ways you can say no that feel comfortable. Let's look at a few examples below. Add your own thoughts or change the words so they feel more like you, if you want!

1. "I really like you, but I don't think I'm ready for that yet."

2. "I'm flattered that you think about me that way, but I just don't feel comfortable with this."

3. "I appreciate your confidence in asking me, but I don't think we're on the same page. I only wanted to _____ with you tonight."

4. "I think I need more time to see how I feel before doing _____. Let's go for a walk and talk more tonight instead."

5. "I'm sorry, I'm not interested in you in that way. I really like you as a friend, but I don't really want anything more than that."

6. "I know it can be hard to put yourself out there, and I know it can suck to hear no, but unfortunately I'm not interested. But thanks for asking and for being respectful."

If someone isn't being respectful with you, it's important to be extremely firm and clear with them if it seems safe to do so. Don't worry about seeming rude—it's your right to say no and to be in full control of your choices with your body, and this person isn't being respectful of you. You're entitled to be as firm and clear as you want to or need to at any point, for any reason. What you say in this situation, if it feels safe to do so, might sound more like this:

1. "Stop—I am not comfortable and I don't want to do this."

2. "No, I'm not interested."

3. "Stop touching me, I am not consenting to this."

4. "This is not consent. I need you to stop right now."

5. "No—I don't want to do this with you. I'm going home now."

6. "I am not consenting to this, and if you keep doing this, that is assault. Stop now."

Practice saying some of these things to yourself or out loud to a friend or partner. You can even practice in a mirror. If we're comfortable saying these words by ourselves, it can make it less scary to say them in a moment of intimacy. It can help you find the words you need if you're ever actually in that situation.

It's important that we also learn to feel comfortable with saying no and turning people down—even people we may really like or even love. Just because you like or love someone doesn't mean you have to be sexually intimate with them if you don't want to or if you don't feel ready. And if they're worth your love and friendship, they'll respect your boundaries and your decisions. Let's practice a bit right now.

Setting Boundaries and Facing Fears

Close your eyes, and imagine someone you really like asking you to be intimate with them in a way that you aren't ready for right now. Now, picture yourself setting a boundary and saying no to them. Try some of the above suggestions for how to communicate your boundary to them. Imagine their reaction in your mind—even your worst-case scenario. And then notice how you feel as you imagine this.

1. Did you notice yourself feeling hesitant or confident as you imagined saying no? If you didn't feel confident, what do you think your fear was? What made you feel unsure or nervous?

2. Then, as you pictured the other person's response to you, did you still feel strong and secure in your decision? Or did you imagine yourself wanting to make them feel better, or changing your mind in order to change their reaction?

We can sometimes be caught off guard by how tough it can feel to say no to a person or to set a boundary—especially with people we like or love. Many of us are taught to not hurt people's feelings, to be nice and kind, and to go with the flow. But those expectations can't apply to sexual intimacy. Sexual intimacy is a very personal, vulnerable thing. You should never feel like you have to bend or shift from what feels best or right for you to make someone else feel better. These are firm and clear boundaries that every person is entitled to have.

There are also a number of reasons why setting these boundaries can feel difficult. It can be helpful to dig into some of our own personal fears or worries to see where our tough spots might be. What do you find yourself most sensitive to when it comes to setting boundaries? Here are some common worries people have:

1. Worries about how the other person will react

    - The person might stop being your friend or stop liking or loving you.

    - The person will get mad or criticize you for setting a boundary or saying no.

    - The person won't listen to you if you say no. They'll keep pushing or asking anyway.

2. Worries about how you'll feel afterward

    - You'll feel guilty for "hurting someone's feelings" after the fact.

- You'll later regret not being intimate with this person, and you don't want to feel like you missed out. What if the opportunity doesn't come up again?

3. Worries about how your peers or friends will react

- People will talk about the situation after the fact and judge you negatively.

First, while hopefully a kind, respectful response from a partner or friends is more likely than some of these responses, we don't want to dismiss them in hopes they'll never happen. Because we unfortunately know that they do happen at times. So, to protect ourselves, our brains can focus on the possibility, however small, that those bad things *could* happen. Remember, your brain wants to keep you safe —and sometimes, "safety" is as much about avoiding rejection or keeping things from escalating as it's about not doing something we don't want to do. And that can sometimes send you into those middle-floor responses we talked about in the last chapter. Our defense systems engage if we feel helpless or like we don't know what to do. But we don't want to let that worry stop us from confidently setting a boundary from a top-floor place of clarity (if we're safe enough to do so).

The good news is, our brains can overcome our fears better when we've thought through some solutions ahead of time—even the worst-case scenarios. So how do we deal with some of these worries if they *do* happen? Let's start with number 1—worries about how the other person will react.

First things first—know that the other person's reaction isn't your fault. You don't have to own the other person's emotions or change your boundaries to accommodate their reaction. If someone stops being your friend or gets mad at you because you've set a boundary with them, it's not your fault. It's especially hard if you care about the person, but if someone doesn't respect something as important as sexual boundaries, we may have to give up the story we told ourselves about that person. And they didn't deserve our friendship in the first place.

If you're with someone—even someone who seems awesome and cool—and they actually stop liking you or get angry if you refuse to do something intimate with them, then how cool is that person, really? Is that the kind of person you want to be with? Remind yourself of your worth—you deserve respect, always.

So if someone does get mad or stops being your friend, they're showing you new information about themselves and how able they are to respect you as a person. Empower yourself by knowing that you're worth putting yourself first. You can say, "I'm sorry you feel that way, but this is my choice." Communicate your boundaries clearly, and remember that even if they try to make you feel differently, you have done the right thing by listening to yourself and what feels right for you, even in the face of a difficult response.

Sometimes we might feel unsafe to say no and communicate boundaries assertively. If that's the case, try to create space from the person instead. You might excuse yourself to the bathroom, or even say that you feel sick and that you need to go throw up. Then leave the space, and call for help from someone you trust—a friend, parent, or helpline. We'll talk more about this in chapter 6.

What about number 2 on the list of worries—worries about how you'll feel afterward? Remember, if someone is hurt or upset, remind yourself that they're entitled to their emotions—but that their emotions are their responsibility to work through and learn and grow from, not yours. You don't have to feel guilty at all. And the feeling of being left out? If you do eventually want to be intimate with someone and they're interested in you, there will probably be another opportunity.

Lastly, number 3 on the list—fears of how friends or peers will react. If people judge you for your own personal sexual decisions, remind yourself that this also isn't about you. People often make judgments based on their own issues and stuff they're working through, which have nothing to do with you. Remember that the right people who respect and care for you will appreciate that you're true to yourself. There's a quote that goes like this: "Be who you are and say what you feel, because those who matter don't mind, and those who mind don't matter."

You Are Worth It

No matter what, you are worthy and deserving of someone who will listen to you and respect you. Let's come up with a few little mantras to help you always remember this. You can say these things to yourself even in those moments of self-doubt or fear. They'll remind you that the only people who deserve to be intimate with you are those who respect you. And they'll also remind you that someone who's disappointed with a decision you make about who you're intimate with is responsible for dealing with their own emotions, not you.

Here are a few examples.

1. A person who cares for me wouldn't want me to do something I don't really want to do. I'm not going to be intimate with someone who doesn't care about my feelings.

2. It's my body; I get to decide. If someone doesn't listen to me, I'm not going to change my mind to make someone else happy.

3. If they're someone worth being intimate with, they're going to respect me. I deserve respect.

4. If they're upset with my decision to say no, that's their stuff to deal with, not mine. I know what's right for me and I'm going to be true to myself.

5. My body, my rules. If someone doesn't like that, they can find someone else to be with, because I deserve someone who respects my comfort and how I feel.

6. If someone only sees me as a body they want, that person is missing what's really important. I want someone who respects all of me.

Choose one or more of the reminders above that feel like they fit. You can tweak them to suit you if you want, or you can come up with a few of your own! Find the words and the vibe that fits your personality and what speaks to you. Have your mantra ready in your mind to offer support whenever you need it. It will help strengthen you in tough moments.

These mantras can help you be assertive. But sometimes, even when we communicate clearly, a situation can still feel unsafe and it can still feel hard to find your words. For more on that type of situation, see the full discussion in chapter 6.

That being said, practicing these words ahead of time can strengthen your ability to find them when you need them, even when it feels really tough. When we get nervous, the more familiar we are with things, the easier they are to do and say (for example, practicing a speech before a class presentation helps you perform better even when you're nervous). So keep practicing these phrases to continue to build your comfort and confidence.

Your Sexual Rights

Along with a mantra, let's look at your rights when it comes to sex—what you are entitled to, no matter what, no matter with whom, and no matter the circumstances. Consider putting a copy of this list (inspired by Maltz 2001) somewhere you'll always have access to—maybe a note in your phone or a picture in your phone's gallery.

You have a right to:

- A partner who is respectful, kind, and considerate of you and your choices

- Ask questions and communicate with a partner about sex without shame, and with respect for your privacy

- Experience sexual pleasure and explore your sexuality safely and enjoyably

- Develop and explore your own sexuality based on your preferences and your orientation

- Develop, explore, and have your own feelings, opinions, and beliefs about sex and sexuality

- Set your own boundaries and limits around your sexual experiences

- Be in control of what sexual contact happens to you: who, what, when, where, why, and how

- Be asked for consent before anything sexual or intimate is done with you or to you

- Say no to anything that ever feels uncomfortable or unsafe or unwanted at any time, for any reason

And of course, remember that any partner you have will also be entitled to these very same rights. We all are.

DEALING WITH REJECTION: GETTING READY FOR "NO"

When we're setting boundaries with another person, our focus is on what *we* want and what's right for *us*. However, when we're the person making a sexual suggestion to another person, what *we* want and what's right for *us* is no longer the priority—the priority is now making sure our partner is on the same page, and that we have their true and total consent.

And of course, sometimes that involves finding out that the answer is no. We might have to deal with rejection. And that's okay! We *want* our partners to be open and honest with us. Having the opportunity to respect another person's wishes and boundaries actually *builds trust* and can deepen relationships and friendships.

Our partner might not be ready or interested in our idea of what we'd like to do with them sexually. We have to be ready and willing to calmly, gracefully, and compassionately let go of what we wanted and meet our partners where they're at. Just like we'd want them to do for us too! Let's explore how to do this.

Disappointment: When It Happens to You

The signs that a partner doesn't want to do what you want to do may be obvious (like saying no) or more subtle and nonverbal (for example, getting quiet, changing the subject, looking uncomfortable, or making a joke), like we explored in chapter 3. And we have to know how we ourselves might react if someone tells us no. We're in charge of and responsible for our own reactions and emotions in that moment.

Getting rejected or turned down will happen to all of us at some point once we've started exploring sexual intimacy. And before that happens, we ideally want to get a full sense of how we might react. What would it feel like to get rejected? How might we handle it? How would we want to react and what would we do next?

Before asking for consent, it's important to have a plan of how to switch gears safely and calmly if your partner doesn't want to do what you were hoping to do. If you don't think you could handle and honor a "no" from someone, you're putting yourself and your partner in real danger. So let's get cozy with this uncomfortable feeling of rejection.

Author and safe sex educator Mike Domitrz (2016) offers some great advice on how to handle rejection. He suggests saying something like this: "Then I'm so glad I asked you, because the last thing I would want to do is make you uncomfortable." Saying something like this helps the other person know that their consent matters, that you're respectful of their feelings, and that it's safe for them to express their true comfort level. A win on every level! It may even bring you closer together—either as friends or as romantic partners. Trust is built in moments like this, and everyone wants and deserves to be respected.

Let's practice this in an imagined scenario. You can grab a pen and paper if it helps to jot your thoughts down.

Picture the person you're most interested in right now. Pick someone who gets your engine revving and your heart racing a bit. Now, imagine you're at a party with this person, and you're both flirting. Imagine how excited you're feeling! Imagine what might be going through your mind about what you hope you could do together. It feels like all your dreams might be coming true.

Now imagine that you reach out and touch this person's arm, and say to them, "I really like you; can I kiss you right now?" and suddenly their smile falters a bit, and they hesitate. Their eyes change ever so slightly. They say, "Umm…" and pause. Imagine yourself in that moment—the real, honest disappointment you might feel inside. Let yourself feel it. Notice: What emotions come up? Where do you feel those emotions in your body—your chest, stomach, throat, or somewhere else? Jot down what that feels like, and what other thoughts might be going through your mind.

Now, take a big, deep breath. And then a few more breaths. And then imagine yourself putting your own thoughts and desires on a shelf in your mind, pulling your hand back from that person's arm, and smiling at them in understanding, communicating to them that you respect and appreciate their hesitation and boundaries. Imagine yourself saying to them, "Hey, I just had to ask. I'm having so much fun with you. But the last thing I would ever want to do is to make you uncomfortable. More than anything I just like spending time with you."

Imagine this being truly okay with you, because you respect this person—you respect *all* people—even if it hurts to feel rejected. You remind yourself that this hurt is your own feeling to deal with—not the other person's responsibility. You make a promise to yourself that you'll take your time to heal and work through it on your own later on if you need to—but that right now, you'll respect and honor this person's desires and signals. You know you want them to be happy even if that means not being intimate. You know there are other people and opportunities out there, and there will be other situations where you and a partner will both feel equally excited and into it.

Now, as you finish playing this scenario out in your head, take a moment and notice:

1. Was there anything about this that felt challenging, or difficult? Was there a moment you felt you wanted to do or say something different than what's in this script?

2. What was the hardest part for you? Did you feel the urge to try to talk the person into something? Did you feel mad or upset that you had to stop right away when they said no? Try

to be honest with yourself, because this is where we can learn and grow. This stuff isn't always easy—there are a lot of emotions involved. But it's important that we think about it.

3. If you had any trouble imagining yourself going through this scenario calmly and coolly without trying to change the person's mind, try to take a moment and notice why that might be. What might you be afraid of? Is there an old hurt or another influence in your life (like a parent, friend, or past romantic partner) that makes you feel like you have to behave differently for some reason? Take a moment and notice this—and think about what you truly want for *yourself*. Who do *you* want to be, and how do *you* want to act?

Let's look at a quick example about a guy named Mark, who thought about this question himself.

Mark was really excited about the idea of making out with Javier—he had thought about it for weeks. But he knew Javier might not feel the same way, so as an exercise, he tried picturing himself asking Javier if he wanted to head to the couch and make out with him while they were on a date.

He pictured Javier hesitating and looking nervous. Mark knew this was a sign that Javier didn't have the same idea—that he wasn't ready to make out, or maybe he didn't want to. Mark knew he should change the subject or offer to just watch a show together instead. But when Mark visualized doing this, he felt a voice in the back of his head laughing at him. He felt ashamed and embarrassed and unwanted, which felt horrible. He could feel himself wanting to try to keep asking Javier, trying to change his mind. But he didn't like how that felt. He knew that he didn't want to be the kind of person who had to talk someone into something they weren't ready for. He knew that wasn't right. He knew that he wanted to be the kind of guy he could be proud of, knowing that he acted and reacted with integrity. So where was this laughter in his head coming from?

As he thought more about it, he realized that he heard his friends in his head, laughing and joking about him the next day after his date with Javier. He was worried they would try to make him feel like he should have been more "manly" and aggressive, and that it was embarrassing to get turned down. But then Mark thought more about it. Who did he really want dictating his love life and his sexual experiences—himself, or his friends? He knew the answer immediately. He didn't want anyone else to make his choices for him. And then he realized that he didn't agree with those friends, anyway. That's not how to live or to act, and that's not what's truly "manly" anyway— respect and confidence are manly, not desperation and force.

And so he imagined what he might say to his friends in response to their laughter. He imagined saying to them, "You guys are going to have a real hard time finding someone who actually likes you if this is how you see other people. Me? I'm going to be fine. Maybe you should think about why you think this is funny—because this isn't funny; it's normal to respect another person." And if they kept laughing, he pictured himself calmly and confidently walking away, smiling at the knowledge that he acted and reacted in a way that was true to himself and who he wanted to be, even if it was difficult at first.

If you can picture yourself doing this exercise, like Mark did, and you're truly able to see this movie play out in your mind, and you're able to see yourself acting safely and appropriately in the face of disappointment and rejection, then you're totally on the right track.

Give yourself a few other imagined scenarios where things don't work out—imagine all your worst-case scenarios of being turned down. Think about what you might feel, do, or say. Keep safety and respect as the priority. You absolutely must be comfortable and confident with these imagined scenarios before you try to be intimate with people in real life.

At the same time—don't let this exercise discourage you from talking to people and putting yourself out there in a safe and healthy way once you're ready! You never know what could happen if you try talking to someone you like—as long as you know you're ready to always, *always* respect the other person's wishes and look for their signs and signals, whether yes *or* no.

However, if you're feeling so scared of rejection that you're not willing to look for and respect your partner's "no" signs, then you aren't yet ready to be sexually involved with someone. Take a bit more time on your own to explore why this might be, and talk to someone you trust about these feelings—a parent, friend, mentor, or counselor might be able to help. As you figure out your feelings, you'll find yourself ready to engage in total consent, which is the only real way to have healthy, happy, safe, and enjoyable sexual interactions.

THE IMPORTANCE OF HEALTHY RELATIONSHIPS

As we think about setting boundaries and dealing with rejection, different *relationship dynamics*—patterns of behavior—start to come up. How a relationship functions can have a big impact on what conversations around consent look like. Certain relationship dynamics can help people feel safe expressing what they want or don't want.

When we communicate in healthy ways and build trust with each other, we feel safer. When we feel safe with a partner, we're more likely to be able to communicate our true feelings and stay in that top floor of the Survival House where we can be intimate with people. As we think about setting boundaries and dealing with rejection, we should also think about the types of relationships that create safety and healthy communication. We want to create relationships where we truly feel safe to express ourselves, and where we're confident that our boundaries will be respected. What do healthy relationships really look like?

The first element that helps us feel safe in any relationship is *trust*. But this concept can actually be a little more complicated than people first assume—so let's break down what trust really is, so we know what to look for.

Trust

Brené Brown (2015) outlines the seven most important aspects that help build trust in a relationship. They form the acronym BRAVING. Remember, each partner in a relationship is equally responsible for these elements.

B—Boundaries. Trust is built with a partner when each person respects what the other person says is okay or not okay for them. If you set a boundary with a partner and they respect it, it creates trust between you. For example, if you tell someone, "Sorry, I don't have time to talk on the phone tonight," and instead of getting mad, they say, "Cool, thanks for letting me know, let's talk tomorrow," this creates trust and respect between you.

R—Reliability. When your partner does what they say they'll do, this builds trust. You know your partner is reliable and dependable.

A—Accountability. When your partner holds themselves accountable for screwing up, this builds trust that your partner can be responsible for their part of the relationship dynamics. You each own your mistakes, apologize, and make repairs with each other when that's needed.

V—The Vault. This is when your partner respects "the vault" of intimate details or knowledge you've shared. They don't share information about you that they don't have permission to share. This also applies to people outside of your relationship—respect is given and shown for all people's rights to privacy.

I—Integrity. When your partner upholds the same values and morals, no matter the circumstances, this builds trust and safety. For instance, they don't treat you terribly during a fight but kindly when you're getting along. Integrity would be treating you kindly at all times, even if you're in a disagreement. You behave consistently. Both of you choose what's right over what might be more fun, faster, or easier.

N—Nonjudgment. When your partner makes a safe space for you to be your true self, without shaming you or judging you for who you are, this creates safety and trust. You both can ask for what you need without judgment.

G—Generosity. When your partner first assumes the best about you before assuming the worst, with a generous heart and spirit, it creates safety and trust and makes communication stronger and easier.

Each of these aspects can be important to notice and think about as you envision being intimate with a partner. If an aspect is missing, you may have more trouble communicating about consent and feeling safe to speak up about your true feelings. The safer you both feel, the easier it'll be for you both to be happy and excited. And the easier it will be to communicate about and enjoy intimacy if and when you're both ready.

Healthy Communication

It's also important to notice how we talk to each other during disagreements. There are four main dynamics that can make us feel judged, hurt, and unsafe with a partner: criticism, defensiveness, contempt, and stonewalling. And there are four ways we can combat these problems: gently starting up and complaining without blame, accepting responsibility, refocusing on connection, and deep breathing (Gottman and Silver 1999).

How we treat each other when we disagree can set the stage for how safe we feel communicating about difficult things, like consent, rejection, and boundaries. Let's have a look at the problem dynamics and how we fix them. To explore these ideas, let's use an example of a couple who are in a disagreement about a party, where one partner spent time outside with their friends, while the other was alone in the house with everyone else.

Problem 1: Criticism. In this scenario, one partner might say to the other, "You always pick your friends first; you never think of my feelings at all."

When we criticize another person (for example, by making a global statement about how awful they are, often using words like "you always" or "you never"), we can make them feel disrespected or devalued. This can make them feel like it isn't safe to communicate how they feel. So what do we do instead?

Solution 1: Gently start up, and complain without blame. Instead of harshly criticizing, gently work up to difficult topics with a partner. For example, you might say, "Hey, do you have a moment to talk about something a bit tough that has been on my mind since yesterday?" Then, you can complain without blaming the other person, by keeping to the specific problem.

In the party example, one partner might say, "It hurt my feelings yesterday when you left me alone at the party for so long to hang out with your friends. I wish you would balance your time between us a bit better next time, or invite me along."

Problem 2: Defensiveness. In the party situation, if the other partner was defensive, they might say, "No, I didn't. It was only for a few minutes. And besides, you did the same thing to me at the last party."

When we disagree, sometimes we'll go on the defensive and block out criticism or complaints by deflecting them. Unfortunately, this can be unhealthy and shut down communication between partners. So what can we do instead?

Solution 2: Accept responsibility. In a disagreement, we can almost always see how something we did—even a small thing—might have bothered our partner. To avoid the unhealthy pattern of dismissing your partner's feelings, accept the responsibility that's appropriate. This might sound like, "Yes, I was outside with them for a bit. I'm sorry that made you feel alone. I can try to make sure I bring you along next time, or not spend so long with them next time."

Problem 3: Contempt. Contempt is shown by things like eye-rolling, sarcastic and biting comments (like "Oh, here we go again, the crazy train is leaving the station"), or disrespectful labeling or name-calling (like "There you go, overreacting and being ridiculous again").

If an argument gets rolling, and criticism and defensiveness are flying back and forth, often one or both partners can slip into the toxic dynamic of contempt. This can be very hurtful and can even be a sign of an unhealthy relationship (which we will explore in the next section). What can we do instead?

Solution 3: Refocus on connection. If you feel yourself getting pulled into feelings of contempt for a partner, take a moment to remember why you actually like this person—what made you want to hang out with, date, or be with them in the first place? Remember that a part of you does like or maybe even love them. Agree to shelve the disagreement or discussion until you both feel more connected and grounded. But if the person is treating you unsafely, or there are ongoing toxic fights like this that happen frequently, it may be time to reconsider if this is the right relationship for you.

Problem 4: Stonewalling. Stonewalling is when a person stops talking, stops responding, and shuts the other person out.

If things keep going in a disagreement, one or both partners are likely to be on the middle floor of the Survival House, in fight-or-flight mode. They'll have a lot of adrenaline pumping through them, and if things don't get better or no solution is in sight, they can drop all the way down to the bottom floor, where they start to shut down because they feel trapped or helpless. This can make people stop talking, zone out, or dissociate in the moment. What can we do to help instead?

Solution 4: Deep breathing (physiological self-soothing). Each person needs to stop here and take deep breaths, take a moment, and maybe go for a walk by themselves to get some space and calm down. The goal is to be able to come back to each other and talk calmly again from the top floor of the house, where each partner feels safer to communicate.

Now that you know these four problems and their solutions, you can keep an eye out for communication dynamics that are healthy and that create feelings of safety, and for those that don't. The safer it feels to communicate and express yourself with a partner—even, or especially, with the tough stuff—the safer and better you both will feel during moments of consent and intimacy. Trust and healthy communication underpin every interaction in a relationship—including consent.

Knowing how to build healthy communication and safety will help as we move into the next section of the book, where we'll look at how to apply all of these skills as we explore dealing with boundaries and rejection. We'll also explore some of the best ways to ensure that you and your partner are feeling safe and secure in intimate moments—before, during, and after an intimate encounter—for total and true consent.

Unhealthy Relationships

Now that you know some of the patterns that can make a relationship healthy—the BRAVING aspects that build trust, as well as the four healthy solution approaches to conflict—we should make sure we have a clear outline of relationship behaviors that aren't okay. While we hope our relationships will be healthy, sometimes this isn't the case. We have to know when to walk away for our own safety.

There are some clear warning signs of unhealthy (or even abusive) relationships that we should be aware of. They include behaviors like the following:

- Extreme jealousy or insecurity, which may include trying to control who you talk to or who you're friends with

- Isolating you from family or friends—making you feel like you should only see, talk, or hang out with them, or saying things like, "I'm the only person who truly cares about you"

- Making false accusations—telling you that you're cheating or lying as a way to control you, or to get you to stop doing something or talking to someone

- Gaslighting—doing something disrespectful or hurtful, and then making you feel like you're crazy for feeling hurt or getting upset about it

- Constantly putting you down—name-calling, insulting, or belittling you

- Explosive anger—even if a person apologizes afterward, if someone makes you feel unsafe or scared when they get really angry, this can be a big warning sign. You should always feel safe with your partner.

- Physically hurting you in any way—hitting, punching, slapping, kicking, pushing, biting, grabbing, shaking, squeezing, choking, holding or restraining, or anything that feels forceful or unsafe

- Possessive behavior—if someone tries to make you feel like they own you because they're in a relationship with you, saying things like, "I'll hurt anyone who even looks at you—you're mine"

- Checking your phone, social media, private messages, or email without permission

- Controlling behavior—telling you what to do often or all the time, what to wear, how to act, or what to do with your life or time

- Pressuring or forcing you to have sex or do sexual things— this isn't consent and should *never* happen in any kind of relationship. Dating a person doesn't give them the right to your body.

Remember also that most unhealthy relationships don't always start out that way—many feel great, wonderful, loving, and exciting in the beginning. But the hard truth is that sometimes things can change in a bad way—even if the start of a relationship was really amazing. If any of the behaviors listed above become a part of a relationship you're in, then it isn't the kind of relationship you want to stay in. These are signs of abuse in a relationship.

It can be hard to step back from a relationship with someone we really like or even love. And sometimes we can truly care about someone who hurts us. But remember, we *always* deserve to be treated with respect and kindness. And if you walk away from a relationship with a person who isn't showing you kindness, it doesn't mean you don't care about them. It means you're choosing to also love and care about yourself. Loving and caring about yourself can sometimes mean not being in a romantic relationship with a particular person. It's okay to miss something—but at the same time, to know that you don't want it back.

If you ever find yourself in a situation like this, I encourage you to talk to a trusted adult, teacher, or counselor about it to get some support. You haven't done anything wrong, and you aren't in trouble—but it can help to talk to someone who can help figure out what to do so that you can stay safe.

Whether you've been in an unhealthy relationship before or not, let's be proactive and think through how you might handle that type of situation. Having a plan and knowing your own boundaries can make it easier to spot trouble. These questions can help you think about what you might want to do.

Let's look at both how we might know if a person has truly and safely earned our trust, and what to do if they aren't treating us in a safe or healthy way.

Relationships: Handling the Tough Stuff

1. What are things that scare you or that you feel nervous about in a relationship or about physical or emotional intimacy with a partner? How might you build trust and safety with a safe partner to handle these worries?

2. Why should someone never call you names, tell you that you aren't attractive, or make you feel bad about yourself? How would you know those things weren't true, even if someone you loved said them to you?

   - How would you react if that ever happened?

   - Who would you turn to for help if you didn't know what to do?

3. If someone were pressuring you to do something you didn't want to (like staying out past curfew, hanging out instead of studying, doing something sexual), what would you say?

   - What if the person who was pressuring you was someone you really admired or even loved? How would you handle it?

4. What would you do if you ever found yourself in a relationship where someone was saying unhealthy things about you or to you? How would you handle it? Why would you want to handle it in that way?

    ▪ Do you think you would feel differently in a long-term relationship or a brand-new relationship? Why? What would the differences be?

    ▪ Who could you go to for help if you needed to?

5. How do you feel about not being in a relationship? Does being alone feel scarier to you than being in a relationship with a person who doesn't treat you well?

    ▪ If so, why? Who can you talk to about this to get some support?

    ▪ What other kinds of things could you do with your time and focus if you aren't in a relationship?

Let's look at an example about someone named Alisha, and what she did in a tough situation.

Alisha started dating Fynn, and everything started off amazing. He was attentive, caring, a great listener, and really wanted the best for her. He did such thoughtful things. They checked in constantly—with good morning and good night texts, and updates throughout the day. Things were truly amazing.

But as they dated a little bit longer, some of the initial excitement wore off. Alisha had to focus on school and make sure that she got her homework done. She also had commitments to the volleyball team and work on the weekends. Fynn was busy too—but he kept wanting to check in as often as when they first started dating. Alisha did her best, but texts every hour or two were getting really tough, especially when she wasn't supposed to have her phone out at work. She told Fynn the reasons she couldn't text all the time, but he was very hurt and upset. She did her best, but it was still a bit of a strain.

When Alisha told Fynn she would be out of town one weekend for her best friend's birthday party, he blew up at her. He told her she was already so busy all the time, and now she was going away for a whole weekend? He told her he didn't want her to go, or he would break up with her. She was heartbroken. Fynn meant so much to her—she couldn't lose him. So she called her friend and told her she couldn't go to the party, faking sick. She and Fynn hung out that weekend, and everything seemed great again.

Until the next week when Alisha's phone went off while she was watching a movie with Fynn, and a message flashed up on the screen. Fynn grabbed her phone and made her open it and show him who the message was from. She said it was from a guy friend of hers. Fynn didn't believe her when she told him the guy was just a friend. He told her to tell that friend not to talk to her again. He told Alisha not to talk to guys on social media anymore—he felt it was disrespectful to him. Alisha couldn't bear to hurt Fynn, so she agreed. As soon as she sent messages to her friends telling them to stop talking to her, Fynn calmed right down, snuggled up, and told her how amazing and loyal and strong she was. Of course she was doing the right thing, she thought.

But as the months wore on, Alisha realized that slowly she wasn't talking to anyone else at all. Her friends were all mad at her for not talking to them. Alisha finally realized that something wasn't right. She started to think about how many changes had truly occurred since she and Fynn first started dating. Even though it was hard to believe, and she wished from the bottom of her heart that it could have been different, she saw that her relationship with Fynn wasn't healthy or balanced. Even though things had started so well, they were very different now.

Alisha wasn't sure what to do at first. But she knew she did have to tell someone. She decided to talk to her guidance counselor at school—she knew they were trained to help with things like this.

As she told the guidance counselor her story, she was reassured that indeed, this kind of behavior unfortunately wasn't healthy and that Fynn wasn't treating her with trust, respecting her boundaries, or allowing her healthy independence in a relationship. The counselor talked with Alisha about any risks she might be worried about if she ended the relationship with Fynn—had he ever threatened her or physically hurt her, or anyone else? Alisha said no. Even if he had, though, the counselor let her know there were still lots of ways to safely exit the relationship that she could help her with.

The counselor helped Alisha pick a method for exiting the relationship that felt right for her, but also safe. Alisha decided to do it over the phone, when she knew Fynn's parents were home so whatever reaction he had, someone would be there.

And though it was hard, and Alisha already knew she missed Fynn and the good parts of their relationship, she knew she had to move on and find a dynamic that was healthy. If she ever found herself in a situation like this again, she realized that she would end things sooner, paying attention to her boundaries. She realized she wanted a relationship where things felt equal, where there was trust, and where someone listened to her perspective even on tough topics. She realized she deserved that—and so does everyone.

If you find yourself in a situation like Alisha's, know that there are always options for help and support. You deserve someone who will treat you with respect and kindness. A healthy relationship— long term or short term—underpins conversations around consent. We should feel safe and respected in every way by the person we're engaging with.

So, now we know which relationship dynamics can help us feel safe, and which aren't safe. We have a sense of what consent is, what it looks like, and the different aspects of our body and brain that can impact how we may respond in the moment. Let's put it all together and draw a full picture of consent in every dimension—legally, emotionally, socially, and physically.

PUTTING IT ALL TOGETHER

As we learned, total consent isn't just a question and answer scenario. It isn't just asking, "Do you want to…?" followed by a "yes" or "no." *Consent is a complete way of approaching sexual intimacy.* The following information brings together everything we've learned so far.

In this section, we'll bring together the aspects of our own sexuality, interests, and preferences we explored in chapter 1; the legal definition of consent we established in chapter 2; the information regarding communication and the Survival House that we learned in chapter 3; and the practical aspects of setting boundaries, dealing with rejection, and the importance of healthy relationships that we learned about earlier in this chapter. This gives us four different aspects to consider when we look at total consent: the legal, emotional, social, and physical levels. Let's have a look at each!

Legal Consent and Safety

Remember that legal rules are in place for everyone's safety. So we always start here, taking a quick inventory of the legal basis of consent, and asking ourselves if each person feels in control of the who, what, when, where, why, and how of everything that's happening. Consider these questions before you plan on being involved with someone in an intimate way.

Check first about capacity to consent:

- Is the person I'm with alert and fully conscious of their actions? Do they have the capacity to consent, regarding their age and vulnerability—and do I?

- Am I fully conscious, alert, and sober enough to make my choices, and is my partner?

- Do I have power over this person that would make them afraid to say no because they're afraid of a negative reaction I could have, or vice versa? Do they have any power over me that's making me feel uncomfortable?

Check for affirmative, freely given HOT SPICE:

- **H**—Honest:

  - Have I thought about what I'm comfortable with and what my boundaries are—and has my partner had a chance to do the same?

  - Do we agree on what this intimacy might mean for our relationship?

  - Do we both want to do this—with no pressure or expectations if we don't?

- **O**—Ongoing:

  - Am I ready and willing to think about boundaries I might want to sets with my partner?

  - Am I ready and willing to deal with rejection, respecting the boundaries my partner sets with me?

  - Are we checking in with each other at each stage and each step of what we're doing?

- **T**—Talked-about:

  - Have I clearly communicated what I want to my partner?

- Have I communicated what I don't want to my partner?

- Has my partner communicated what they want to me?

- Has my partner communicated what they don't want to me?

- Is there a verbal aspect to our consent? Do words and body language match?

- **S—Specific:**

  - Do we agree on what we'll be doing—the who, what, when, where, why, and how of this sexual interaction?

- **P—Present-moment:**

  - Has consent been given right now, in this moment, by this partner?

  - Am I making my choices based on the information from this moment—and not on an unspoken idea, or some hope of how things might change in the future (like the hope that a friendship might turn into a relationship)?

- **I—Informed:**

  - Have I disclosed my true age to my partner?

  - Have I shared my actual relationship status with my partner?

  - Have we talked about what contraception or protection we're both comfortable using (condoms, the pill, and so on)?

- Have I been honest with my partner about any STI risks that I'm aware of? Have my partners been honest about this with me? (We'll discuss contraception and STIs more in chapter 5.)

- C—Changeable:

  - Do I feel like I can say no or change my mind with this partner, even once things get going, and vice versa?

  - Am I allowing my partners the space they need to make the decisions that are right for them at this moment in time?

  - Am I willing to look for boundaries and signs of "no," even when things are exciting or arousing?

- E—Enthusiastic:

  - Are my partners engaged and responsive in what we're doing? Are they showing ongoing signs of enthusiastically participating in this with me, and vice versa?

Once we've considered the legal dimensions of consent, we can start to look at the nuances of emotional, social, and physical safety. Let's look first at the emotional side of things.

Emotional Safety

We want to make sure our partners feel emotionally safe with us—and that we feel safe with them. We shouldn't make our partners feel like they have to please us in order for us to stay with them or stay in a relationship with them. And we don't want to feel like we have to do certain things or respond in certain ways to keep another person happy, either.

We each need to be responsible for our own emotions, including disappointment about rejection, so that if our partner doesn't feel ready for something we don't make them feel responsible for our own emotional reaction. Let's look at a few questions you can check in about when you're approaching someone for intimacy and when you're being approached.

Asking for Intimacy: The Emotional Side

- Have you created an emotional environment where your partner truly feels they're able to say no to you? Have you reassured them and encouraged them that you want them to be honest, and only want to do something if they're totally into it and comfortable with their decision?

  - Some emotional environments can make a partner feel "trapped" with no emotional way out—for example, if someone says, "I thought you loved me and that you wanted this too," or something similar. This kind of framing can make someone feel boxed in and trapped emotionally and like their partner doesn't truly respect their opinion on what they would like to do or why.

  - This sense of being boxed in can take a partner from the top floor of the Survival House to the middle or bottom floor—into a yellow- or even a red-light response. No one should feel like there will be conse-quences for not consenting to a sexual act. (If those kind of boxing-in statements or actions seem like something you might do with a partner, think about whether you're really ready for intimacy at this point.)

- Have you pressured your partner in any way—even by accident? Have you tried to talk them into something for any reason? Take an honest inventory of the situation.

  - If you've pressured them in any way, you may have created an unsafe environment for your partner, and they may not be engaging with you on the top floor of their Survival House anymore. They may have slipped into protective responses of freeze, appease, tend and befriend, or other responses that aren't true consent.

  - Make sure you're respecting your partner's right to decide what they are and aren't comfortable with, and let them know that you respect their decision, whatever it is. (And if you don't feel ready to respond to your partner in a way that's respectful and kind if they say no, think about whether you're ready for intimacy at this point.)

Being Asked for Intimacy: The Emotional Side

- Ask yourself, "If I say yes, is it because I really want to do this, or is it because I'm afraid to say no to this person?" Also ask yourself, "Am I doing this now because I'm hoping to get something later in return for this? Like a relationship or some other kind of intimacy?"

  - Consent can only be given for the here and now, and making a decision based on something that we'd like to happen later isn't an ideal way to make a sexual decision. Do an honest inventory with yourself and how you feel, if you can.

- Do you feel like you can't trust how the other person will respond if you reject them or express preferences that are different from theirs? Are you feeling scared?

  - Watch out for freeze, appease, and tend and befriend responses. (If you find yourself slipping into those responses, it may be a sign you should try to create space between yourself and this partner as best you can, like stepping out to the bathroom. See chapter 6 for more discussion of this kind of situation.)

We need to make sure our partners feel safe saying no to us, and reassure them that we'll respect and honor whatever decision they make no matter what. And we need to check that partners make us feel this way as well. We can do this proactively by telling partners up front that we want to truly hear their honest feelings, no matter what, and by communicating our boundaries clearly.

Social Safety

Rejection can be a big trigger for each of us—we have that old evolutionary wiring that tells us that we might die if our tribe of people kicks us out of the club, like we talked about in chapter 3. This can make us more sensitive than we sometimes imagined we would be to social rejection. We want to be conscious of this threat response in a partner or in ourselves so that we can proactively set ourselves up for feelings of safety. Let's look at a few questions we can consider as we think about the social aspect of true consent.

Asking for Intimacy: The Social Side

- Check in about possible social or power dynamics that might be showing up in a relationship with someone else, even outside of the more obvious ones (like a relationship between a teacher and a student). For instance, is the other person influenced by someone they may not want to upset if they didn't get together with you—like a friend who set you up together? Are you in a social position that might feel intimidating to another person in any way?

  - If so, have you given your partner space to safely express their preferences to you, no matter what those preferences happen to be, and no matter what social dynamics might be in play?

- Does your partner feel true social safety if they choose not to engage with you sexually? Have you in any way implied that they won't be cool if they turn you down, or that you'd tell people and "everyone will know" if they say no?

  - If so, you haven't created a socially safe environment for your partner, and you may not have true consent from that person. They might be reacting with middle-floor "appease" responses. Let your partner know that you'll still like them and respect them regardless of their decision. (If you don't feel capable of doing this, think about whether you're really ready for sexual intimacy at this point.)

- Does your potential sexual partner depend on you for anything that might influence their sense of safety if they say no? Do you help them in a study group, work on a project together, drive them to school, or do they depend on you in some other way?

  - Try to make sure your partner doesn't have any sort of dependency—situational, financial, or otherwise—that could make them feel like they can't safely express what they truly do or don't want. If they do depend on you for something, make sure you reassure them and discuss how you wouldn't let their choice affect your other relationships—and stick to that promise.

Being Asked for Intimacy: The Social Side

- Do you feel you can trust your potential partner to treat you with respect whether you engage with them sexually or not? Does this person have a history of treating people well? Do they have a history of behaving with others in ways that make you worry about how they might treat you (like gossiping about others or badmouthing them)?

  - Consider how this might make you feel in a moment of consent with them—is this someone that you trust enough to be intimate with? You might try talking to this person about your worries before proceeding, and see how they react.

- See if the person is able to honor your emotions and respect them—not dismiss them or tell you how you should be feeling. Are they a good listener? Remember the aspects of healthy relationships and trust.

• Are you feeling at all intimidated about another person's popularity, level of attractiveness, or other social position in any way?

- Try to check in and be honest with yourself about how comfortable you are expressing your preferences to this person.

• Watch out for some of the myths we talked about in the second chapter. Notice if you're falling into some of the traps of faulty belief systems (like guys are supposed to do one thing; girls are supposed to do another thing; if someone cool wants to have sex with you then you have to agree because you're lucky; and so on).

- Remember, you have the right to control what happens to you, and the right to say no to something you don't want. You have the right to have sexual intimacy be at the pace at which you're comfortable. No matter what myths come into your head, stay true to yourself and what you deserve. Remember your sexual rights from earlier in this chapter.

In short, we need to try to ensure that social pressures aren't influencing our ability or our partner's ability to make honest decisions about what we want and what we don't want.

Physical Safety

We all should feel in full control of our environment and our ability to leave an intimate situation if we're uncomfortable. We have to allow each other to leave or to stop an activity as soon as signs of discomfort arise, and we need to be able to voice that discomfort if we're feeling it ourselves. Sexual intimacy is a very physical and vulnerable thing, so trust in a physical sense is important.

Remember, we need to each feel in control of the who, what, when, where, why, and how of the situation. Our physical environment and our physical presence with each other can have an impact on how in control we feel. Physical safety often comes down to two things: (1) physical aspects of the environment we're in, like where the room is, how familiar we are with a space, and if we know how to get home; and (2) how our bodies are interacting and positioned, with awareness of possible differences in size or strength. We want to make sure no one feels trapped, even if by accident.

Some environmental aspects can trigger feelings of being trapped and unsafe, depending on each of our comfort levels. These can include closed doors, locked doors, being far away from other people, or feeling someone's physical presence is unsafe. And when we feel like we're not in control or trapped, that can be a big trigger for the Survival House middle- and bottom-floor responses. So we need to continue to be mindful of how we feel about our environment and how our partners feel about it, and check in with each other as we go. We want to continually be communicating, checking in, and watching for signs of enthusiasm, so we can tell if we're all on that top green-light floor.

Asking for Intimacy: The Physical Side

• Consider where you are in the room in relation to your partner, and how they might feel about the physical environment you're both in. Remember that these factors may influence whether your partner feels safe in expressing to you what they really want.

  ▪ Are you between them and a door?

  ▪ Are you and your partner a long way from home, or is there a safe way for them to get home?

  ▪ Are you larger, older, or more experienced than your partner?

• If any of the above are true, or if you're ever unsure how your partner might be feeling, make sure they have physical space to slow down, take stock, and communicate safely with you.

  ▪ Think about creating "slow down" spots in a sexual interaction, where each partner can catch their breath and make sure there is room and time to think about how things are progressing. This will help make sure that your partner can make their decisions from the top floor of the Survival House, rather than from a place of discomfort or panic.

  ▪ Try to create a physically safe environment for your partner, where they know how they can exit a space, how they can get home, and where they can find the physical space to slow down or move away from you if they start to feel uncomfortable.

Being Asked for Intimacy: The Physical Side

- Do you feel physically intimidated by the other person's size or strength?

  - If so, you might let them know that this makes you a bit nervous, and see how they respond. They should respond with concern and a desire for you to feel safe and in control of the situation. They shouldn't laugh at you or belittle you (remember the aspects of healthy relationships). If they do, find space away from this person and get help as best you can. (See chapter 6 for more on this kind of situation.)

- Do you feel you could get up and leave a situation at any time if you felt uncomfortable?

  - If not, you might try to slow things down and create space—let the other person know you're feeling nervous, and see how they respond, like we talked about in the last point.

- Do you have a way to get home that doesn't rely on the other person?

  - As best you can, try to think about having a backup plan or a safe person you can call if you ever feel unsafe. This could be having a ride-sharing app downloaded on your phone, or an agreement with a safe adult in your life that no matter the time of day or circumstances, if you don't feel safe, you can call them and they'll come get you right away.

We should feel in control of the "where" aspect of sexual intimacy. And we should help our partner feel that way, too, continuing to check in with ourselves and our partner that everyone is comfortable and feeling safe with how and where things are happening. Each person should always feel like they're able to leave a situation.

Once we've thought about the legal, emotional, social, and physical aspects of consent, we should be on the right track!

- We've thought about our partner's sense of safety and comfort and our own.

- We've communicated in healthy ways with our partners and encouraged them to do the same.

- We've challenged the myths that may have led us astray.

- We've remembered that it's totally normal and healthy to talk and ask about consent, comfort, and enjoyment every step of the way.

- We've made sure we're confident in what boundaries we want and how we want to set them. And we're equally confident in our ability to handle rejection with grace and respect.

So what might all of this look like, in real life? Let's take a look at an example.

Consent in Action

So how do you put these principles in action in real life? There is no one-size-fits-all model of consent. Getting and giving consent is an ongoing process. And it changes according to the particular situations we're in.

Remember, we want everyone to be on the top floor of the Survival House, where we feel safe and can be intimate. One thing that helps us stay on the top floor is constant communication, checking in, and connecting, in many different small ways. When we're constantly connected with someone, we can stay in tune with them.

We might start with small expressions of intimacy and affection to build trust and communication with each other. This helps make sure everyone feels safe and comfortable communicating their true and honest feelings—what they're okay or not okay with. We should watch for signs and signals from our partner as we use verbal and body language communication to make sure everyone is on the same page.

In a sexual interaction, there can be many small moments of little decisions between partners—little asks, little waits, and little moments of consent or boundaries that each person needs to be constantly aware of. When one person makes a joke, the other person laughs—when one person smiles, the other person smiles back. When we use all of the top-floor parts of our brain and body—our facial muscles, our voice, and our eyes and ears as we listen and speak—these parts of communication can help make sure everyone is feeling safe together.

This flow back and forth is important to feeling safe—if something feels out of rhythm from what we expect, our brains can read that as something feeling off when we're searching for signs of safety. When things move too quickly, we run the risk of jumping way past our or our partner's comfort zone, leading to fear or feelings of not being safe—we didn't stay in a flow together. So we don't want to skip ahead too quickly, especially with a new partner.

But when things move slowly and progressively, with check-ins along the way, we're making sure that everyone is firmly up on the top floor of the Survival House, enthusiastically consenting from that place of intimacy.

In general, if you're *asking for* consent:

- Sexual intimacy, when it escalates, should be slow, with small, progressively intimate steps, and with constant awareness of your partner's level of enthusiasm and engagement. Don't get so caught up in your own world that you forget to check that your partner is into it and feeling good too—the whole point of partnered intimacy is to have a good time together! It feels good to make people feel good! And of course, never just walk up to a person and touch someone in an intimate way without asking, and without establishing a connection and shared interest first.

- Err on the side of caution. If there's a body language signal you're not sure of, use words to check in. If you happen to get both a body language signal and a verbal answer but something still feels off, slow down, stop, take a quick break, or pause to let each other settle and see how you're feeling.

Only move forward with an enthusiastic yes, treating a maybe, silence, or even a hesitant yes as a pause, wait, and stop signal. If you're not sure, you might say, "You seem a bit unsure, and I don't want you to do anything you aren't 100 percent okay with. Why don't we slow down for a second and you can think things over. It's okay if you want to stop."

- Encourage your partner to know and trust that it's safe for them to say no to you, and that you want them to feel safe and comfortable. You might say, "You know I'm totally into you, but I also want you to know that more than that, I want you to feel safe and comfortable. If at any time you don't feel safe or comfortable, just say 'stop' or 'slow down,' and I'll stop or slow down. You get to decide how far and how fast we move—just let me know what you want, and I'll help make it happen."

Here is a possible example of what putting this together can look like:

1. As you're talking with someone, notice the "yes" or "no" signals that we discussed in chapter 3 (check back to that section to refresh yourself if it helps). Don't proceed if you're getting no signals. Just keep chatting as friends, or move on to chat with another person.

2. If someone is showing "yes" signals in their body language, you might try expressing verbal interest. You might say, "I really like you. I'd be interested in getting to know you

better. What do you think?" And then look again to your partner for "yes" or "no" signals—emphasizing their verbal response, but looking for body language to match. If they hesitate, say no, or start making excuses, don't proceed with anything further.

3. If the person expresses mutual interest, you might continue talking and flirting, and then gauge their reaction to a non-sexual physical touch, like on the arm or hand. Look for "yes" or "no" signals of how comfortable they are. If they move away or hesitate, remove the nonsexual touch and just keep chatting as friends. If you aren't sure what signals you're getting, ask the person how they're feeling.

4. If you're still getting "yes" signals from this person, and it feels right based on your relationship and how well you know them, you might now ask directly about a physical, intimate touch that you feel okay with too. Look back to the "Ways to Ask" section in chapter 3 for examples. Encourage the person to be honest with their consent.

In response, if you're *giving* consent:

- If you're providing affirmative consent and you're feeling into it and want something to be happening, providing affirmative, positive signs is good communication. Use words to be clear about what you're okay with and what feels good for you. Sexual intimacy doesn't need to be a silent interaction—noises, words, moans, giggles, or sighs might all be a part of your interaction as you communicate with each other. If you want, you might give verbal encouragement and let your partner know they're on the right track. It can help everyone feel more confident in the moment. You might also verbally tell the other person how you expect things to go and what your boundaries are, being clear about them up front.

- If you're not giving consent, be clear about your boundaries. Try to be kind if your partner is being respectful and kind toward you also. Look back to the "Boundaries and Saying No" section in chapter 4 for examples of how this might sound. When possible and fair, we should try to be respectful of each other's emotions and feelings.

- If your partner isn't being kind or respectful, or isn't listening to your boundaries or signals, try to be even clearer or more assertive if you can. You might also create space from that person by going to the bathroom or getting the attention of someone nearby who may be able to help. We'll talk more about what to do in a situation that starts to feel unsafe in chapter 6.

So, now we know a little bit about what a healthy sexual interaction looks like from beginning to end. We should also zoom out and look at some other aspects that can impact consent—such as how consent grows and evolves with longer-term partners, and topics like contraceptives, alcohol, and drugs. Let's turn to that next!

CHAPTER 5

Some Other Things to Know

So far, we've been approaching consent from the perspective of the first few times that you're intimate with a partner or the times when you're intimate in any new way. When we don't know each other well, we don't always know what exactly to look for or what makes each of us feel safe or unsafe. Going slow and talking things through every step of the way helps make sure everyone feels comfortable, safe, empowered, and in total control of the who, what, when, where, why, and how of sexual intimacy.

You can think of it as like taking the time to put on a seat belt. You may not need it every time, but if you skip that step and something bad happens, you can get hurt badly, and so can your partner. So by going through the proper and respectful steps to ensure everyone is safe, happy, and into it, our risk of getting hurt is reduced.

Now, if we continue to be intimate with the same person multiple times (we of course still do need consent every time), we start to get to know each other better. We've likely already discovered things that feel safe and good with this partner, and things that are off-limits or not okay. We have learned how another person communicates with their body language and verbally. We've started to build trust and comfort at a deeper level. Once we can be more sure of how another person acts and reacts in sexual situations and what to look for in terms of their own unique "yes" and "no" signs, we may start to grow with consent, together.

GROWING WITH CONSENT

There are some more advanced ways to communicate about consent with partners you know well, and with whom you have built a strong foundation of safety. When we have trust, affection, and confidence between partners, this helps us stay on the top floor of our Survival House, where intimacy can happen. We can also communicate more subtly when we know each other better, because we know another person's language and comfort zones.

This is because the first few times we're intimate with someone, we go through all the important steps about ongoing communication. We learn each other's boundaries, what we each want and don't want, and how we each communicate that we're comfortable or uncomfortable with something. This early legwork is super important—and it's often what gives us the ability to grow and evolve with our partners with how we communicate consent. Let's look at some of the ways consent may change over time with trusted and familiar partners.

Implied and/or Nonverbal Consent

When you have increased trust and more intimate knowledge of how you both communicate when you're being physically intimate (when you know what it looks like when each person is really into it), then as you grow together, you might start shifting to more nonverbal consent—relying more on body language during sexual experiences. In these longer-term relationships, you and your partner often start feeling even more safe and comfortable as you share experiences together.

In a healthy long-term partnership, a certain level of sexual intimacy is generally assumed to be healthy and okay within your relationship depending on how you've defined those parameters together. This is *implied consent*. So, to initiate previously agreed-upon sexual intimacy with that romantic partner is generally acceptable— although either partner can turn down the other at any time.

Do remember that just because you've been intimate in the past doesn't mean that you have the right to any further intimacy with a person in the future, so you still need general consent before starting anything with a person—even someone you know well or are in a relationship with. But once you've determined your rhythms in your partnership and you know what to look for, you might need less verbal communication every step of the way than when you first started out together.

This style of consent isn't recommended for very new relationships or if either partner is relatively inexperienced—but it can work well for partnerships where a very good level of trust, understanding, and healthy communication are already present. If you're moving into this territory with a trusted partner, remember to be aware of what you're both feeling and communicating, to still look for any hesitation or changes in your partner's usual enthusiasm, and to stop and check in as needed.

Blanket Consent

As people get older and more sexually experienced, some might prefer to give or receive consent up front, before a sexual interaction starts to occur. This style of asking for and giving consent needs to be agreed upon by both partners beforehand. *Blanket consent* (Vrangalova 2016) is the verbal agreement or understanding that once you've decided together what intimate act you're doing, you agree that everything is good to go within those parameters (for example, vaginal intercourse but not anal intercourse; oral sex but not penetrative sex) and permission doesn't need to be asked for every step of the way—but at any point someone can ask to stop. Partners may also agree on a *safe word*, which if someone says at any point means they want to stop. Partners should still be looking for body language signs that the person is completely and enthusiastically in agreement throughout the encounter.

Remember that even with this strategy, any partner can still withdraw consent *at any time.*

Blanket consent can be risky for less experienced partners, and more risky in general than the total consent model we've been talking about in this book. It's generally only something to consider if you and your partners are quite experienced and confident in knowing what you like and don't like and how to say no assertively. It's generally not recommended if you're just starting out with a new partner, if you're with a partner who may be less experienced than you, or if you're less experienced yourself.

Remember that sometimes people who are less experienced may not even know how they might react to certain kinds of sexual intimacy yet, and they need time to feel and think about their comfort level as things progress. Remember to always err on the side of caution—it takes very little extra time to quickly check in with a partner to see how they're doing and to reassure them that it's okay if they need to stop at any point.

Also remember that if either partner has chosen to consume alcohol or other substances that can even slightly impair decision making (even with longer-term partners), it's recommended to go back to the total consent model that we've talked about earlier— HOT SPICE, verbal, body language, ongoing check-ins, and slow escalation of intimacy—even if partners are experienced with each other. If risk ever increases (as it does with alcohol or other drugs), it's best to use the safest approach possible: the total consent model. Like taking the time to put on a seat belt—just in case—it makes sense to take a few extra moments to make sure everyone is okay and on the same page.

Let's take a little more time to explore how drugs and alcohol can affect consent.

A WORD ABOUT ALCOHOL AND DRUGS

For total consent to happen, every person should have the capacity to think clearly about the who, what, when, where, why, and how of sexual intimacy. This ability can be impaired when drugs or alcohol are used before or during sex. We know that legal consent includes the capacity to consent—someone can't be drunk, blacking out, stumbling, slurring their words, or unconscious. But we also know that there's a lot of space between being completely sober and blacking out. We have to think about the full picture of drug or alcohol use when we think about total consent.

It wouldn't be fair or reasonable to suggest that every sexual interaction should take place when both parties are stone-cold sober. We're all aware that many people use alcohol or drugs in social situations, on dates, and at other points in intimate or sexual relationships. So, how do we approach this from the standpoint of healthy consent?

The boundaries between what's clearly consensual and okay and what isn't can get blurry when drugs and alcohol are involved. For instance, if someone doesn't consent to something earlier in the night when they're sober, but then after two or three drinks they do, is that total consent? Unfortunately, there is no one right answer to this question. We might have total consent, but we also might not. This book can't hope to wrap up this topic in a neat little bow—but we do need to start thinking about it, because it's very important to be aware of it. We do know two things:

1. Reducing or eliminating alcohol or drug use in your sexual encounters is especially important with new partners who you don't know well or haven't been intimate with before—being sexually intimate with someone you've just met after a night of partying with drugs or alcohol is extremely risky, while being intimate with a familiar, longer-term sexual partner in a similar situation might be less risky.

2. If you're not sure how sober a person is or how sober you are, you shouldn't be sexually intimate. Err on the side of caution.

While to ensure full and total consent the only truly safe amount of alcohol is zero, if we choose to use drugs or alcohol, the safest approach is called *harm reduction*. This means that as risk goes up (meaning as more drugs or more alcohol are consumed), we want to be even more careful about how we proceed with a partner. For every drink or drug that is added to an interaction, we have to be that much safer and that much more cautious about how we proceed. Remember that the stakes are high if we guess wrong about consent or are no longer able to communicate consent ourselves—sexual assault and trauma can happen. So we should always err on the side of caution if we're not sure. Let's look at this a little more deeply.

This is what we know for sure: if someone is behaving erratically, yelling, behaving out of character, stumbling, slurring their words, blacking out, or swaying when they stand, then it doesn't matter how enthusiastic they seem in the moment—you should *not* be having any sexual interaction. That person's capacity to consent is quite clearly not there—you should wait until everyone sobers up.

Remember that not everyone looks or acts the same when they're intoxicated. For some people, it's obvious when they're drunk. For others, it can be hard to tell. Some people get quiet, and some people act relatively the same. Unless you've been counting how many drinks you've had and are *very* familiar with your reaction and your partner's reaction to alcohol and tolerance levels, you should err on the side of caution and strongly consider picking a different time to be sexually active. Use the rules of legal drinking and driving laws—one standard-size drink per hour is a rough estimate for most people's legal limit for being and feeling sober.

In general, if someone can't legally drive, they legally can't consent to sexual intimacy. While sometimes in this situation everyone might feel okay about a sexual interaction the next day, there are also times when it doesn't work out, and someone gets seriously hurt. You can think of it as like driving drunk. Although sometimes people drive drunk and make it home without hurting anyone, driving drunk is never okay—because the risk is there, and sometimes people get really hurt. A serious risk is also there when you have sex while intoxicated or with someone who is intoxicated, so you shouldn't do it.

If you choose to skip this rule about consent and alcohol or drugs, you've entered a danger zone—there's no other way around this. If you choose to ignore the risks of using alcohol or drugs while engaging in sexual activity with someone, you're choosing to open yourself up to possible consequences, both legal and emotional. You don't have total consent if your partner isn't "totally there" in their brain—which is how a large amount of alcohol or drugs affects the way our brains work. It makes us not really all there. We need our "total" brains in order to give "total" consent. And the responsibility to look for and get total consent is always on the person initiating the sexual experience—even if everyone's intoxicated.

So when in doubt, just wait. Otherwise, it's like drinking and driving—you might make it home okay, but you also might not. You might seriously injure someone—trauma is serious. And you put yourself at risk of the consequences of the law. Sex and sexual activity can be fun—but it can also be scary, damaging, and traumatizing if real, true, total consent isn't present. And we're often not the greatest judges of this when we're intoxicated—especially with new partners whom we don't know well and may not feel as safe and comfortable with.

The other thing that can make sexual intimacy more dangerous when using drugs and alcohol is an increased risk of using contraceptives incorrectly. Condoms might be put on the wrong way and then flipped around (which can transmit STIs and even sperm), the pill might be forgotten or thrown up (which increases risk of pregnancy), or many other complications might occur. Substances like alcohol, marijuana, and other drugs can impact many aspects of consent and safety.

While we're on the topic of contraceptive and STIs, let's explore more about these aspects of safety and consent. Using contraceptives and communicating about STIs can also be an important part of a total consent conversation. Let's make sure we have the full picture so we can communicate about it safely.

SAFER SEX AND CONSENT

Open and truthful communication about contraception and STIs is part of informed consent (the "I" from HOT SPICE). Along with giving consent to the specific sexual activity, we need to agree on the type of sexual safety used, in terms of contraceptives and STI risks. You have the right to open and clear information from your partners on any risks, including STIs or exposure to other sexual partners if the relationship isn't exclusive. You also have an obligation to share your own information about STIs or other sexual partners before anything intimate happens. Remember, part of our definition of consent is consent to *how* sex happens along with the who, what, when, where, and why aspects.

STIs can be pretty serious. An unplanned pregnancy is also serious and difficult to handle, especially for a young person. For these reasons, we should always be thinking about how to stay as safe as we can when we're sexually active. Ultimately, not having sex at all (abstinence) is the only 100 percent effective method for not contracting STIs and not getting pregnant—but that also isn't very realistic for many people.

So we should definitely know what other options we have to stay as safe and protected as possible. Listed below are several of the methods to prevent pregnancy or STIs. After each method is listed a percentage amount—this is the effectiveness of that approach to preventing pregnancy with *typical use* (as in, what happens in real life with real people, not just in a perfect laboratory, accounting for human error and other factors). Many of these methods may boast higher percentages of prevention on their retail packages, which advertise *perfect use* (Lang 2018).

Barrier Methods

Barrier methods are some of the best preventive measures against STIs and are also quite effective in preventing pregnancy. Barrier methods stop sperm from traveling into the uterus and finding an egg, and they prevent skin-to-skin contact with areas that can transmit STIs:

- The male condom (goes over the penis)—82 percent effective in preventing pregnancy

- The female condom (goes inside the vagina)—79 percent effective in preventing pregnancy

- The dental dam (used for protection during oral sex, not used for pregnancy prevention)

Medication Interventions

These interventions must be taken ahead of sexual activity to reduce the risk of contracting specific STIs. They do not prevent pregnancy.

- Preexposure prophylaxis (or PrEP) is a drug taken ahead of sexual interaction, daily, to prevent HIV. PrEP reduces the risk of getting HIV from sex by about 99 percent when taken correctly (CDC 2019b).

- Vaccinations are available that will help prevent hepatitis A and B and some types of HPV (human papillomavirus). The hepatitis A vaccine is 90 to 97 percent effective (Government of Canada 2018). The hepatitis B vaccine is 80 to 100 percent effective (CDC 2019a), and the HPV vaccine is almost 100 percent effective (National Cancer Institute 2019).

- Other vaccinations may be available in the future. Ask your doctor for any updates.

Hormonal Methods

Hormonal methods only prevent pregnancy. They don't prevent STIs. Contraceptives are taken by women to stop ovulation and thus prevent pregnancy (no egg = no fertilization = no pregnancy). These hormonal options are:

- The birth control pill—91 percent effective in preventing pregnancy

- The patch—91 percent effective in preventing pregnancy

- The ring—91 percent effective in preventing pregnancy

- A shot—94 percent effective in preventing pregnancy

- An implant—99 percent effective in preventing pregnancy

- IUD (intrauterine device; note that not all IUDs use hormones)—99 percent effective in preventing pregnancy

There may be male hormonal options available soon (fingers crossed!), but nothing is publicly available as of the time this book is being published.

There are some other, older birth control options too, like a diaphragm, a cervical cap, or a cervical sponge, each used with spermicide and inserted into the vagina. But these aren't used very often anymore, as other options are much more effective and reliable.

There is also something called the morning after pill (75 to 89 percent effective in preventing pregnancy), which can be used when another method of protection fails (like when a condom breaks unexpectedly). The partner at risk of becoming pregnant must may take it as directed within 72 hours of intercourse, but the sooner it's taken, the more effective it is.

If the possibility of pregnancy applies to you or your partners, you should consider using both hormonal contraception and barrier methods, together, to prevent against *both* pregnancy and STIs. As you think about what feels right for you, you should talk with your doctor about effectiveness levels and what will work best for your lifestyle and health.

STI Screenings and Disclosures

When choosing what method of safer sex is right for you, you might want to consider your partner's sexual history and whether either of you has had, or currently have, other sexual partners. If you're newer partners or don't know each other's sexual history very well, it's wise to use barrier contraception to protect against STIs and to consider getting an updated screening done for a standard STI checkup before sex. Talk to your doctor about what might be best for you as you become sexually active.

Consent and Contraception

Remember that both you and your partner have a right to discuss what contraception you're comfortable with. You shouldn't ever try to force another person to use something they aren't comfortable with—for instance, demanding that your partner use the pill if she doesn't want to. You also shouldn't demand that someone not use a method that they want to use. For instance, you shouldn't demand that someone not use a condom because you don't like it. If you don't feel comfortable or safe, you can choose to walk away. Don't pressure someone to do something they don't want to do. No person's right to freely choose should be impacted. If you don't agree on the methods, then this might not be the right partner for you, and that's okay! Someone else who is a better fit for you will come along. Remember that your health and well-being are always the priority, no matter what.

Like we've said, part of full consent is consent to *how* sex happens. Remember the "S" from HOT SPICE—specific. Which means, for example, that consent to sex with a condom is *not* consent to sex without a condom. If you find that the condom has been removed without your consent during the act, this isn't okay. In fact, it's considered assault, because it isn't what was consented to. If you can safely do so, stop the interaction right away, leave, and talk to someone you trust immediately to get support.

So far, we've been talking about how to make sure consent is always present and that everyone feels safe and comfortable in a sexual situation. But unfortunately, we know that sometimes things can go wrong. When consent isn't present, this is called *sexual assault*. We're going to take the next chapter to learn about what this is and how to handle a situation like this.

CHAPTER 6

What to Do When Things Go Wrong

Sometimes sexual intimacy isn't particularly enjoyable. It can be awkward, uncomfortable, or not pleasurable. This is often a part of learning about sexual intimacy and finding the right chemistry, partners, and activities that you enjoy. Mixed or difficult emotions can sometimes show up after a sexual interaction, too; and, if total consent was present, these emotions don't necessarily mean anything happened that was wrong. It can sometimes just be part of getting to know yourself and learning to make decisions.

But as we think about and practice healthy approaches to consent, we have to acknowledge that there are times when things go wrong. Sometimes, a partner might ignore signals, signs, or outright words. This might have happened to a friend or a family member you know, or it might have even happened to you.

Some of what we talk about in this chapter will be a little heavy. As always, take it at your own pace. Take breaks at any point if you need to. Also, some of the things in this chapter might apply to you, and some might not. Either way, know that it's all important and worth reading about.

When we talk about "things going wrong," when a person doesn't check for our consent or ignores our signs or signals, this means there was a lack of consent. The lack of consent in a sexual encounter is called sexual assault. It's not the same as sex we didn't enjoy. Rather, sexual assault is when that clear, enthusiastic, affirmative consent isn't present or when the other legal aspects of consent aren't present. By understanding what it is and what it can look like or feel like, we can learn to recognize it and figure out what to do about it. We can also learn how to help a friend or someone who looks like they might be in danger of a sexual assault.

Now, let's take a closer look at understanding what sexual assault can look like and feel like, some of the best ways to keep ourselves and others safe, and how to get help if we need it.

SEXUAL ASSAULT

Sexual assault is anything not in alignment with the laws around consent from chapter 2. Sexual assault happens at any point when a person doesn't have our consent to touch our bodies in an intimate way, including pressuring us, coercing us, or not listening to "no" signals and hesitation.

Sexual assault can happen on purpose (with awareness, or planned ahead of time) or without intention (because of a lack of knowledge, or awareness, or negligence). Neither situation is okay. Not knowing how to get consent or what to look for to ensure consent doesn't excuse assault. Negligence or ignorance does not excuse our responsibilities. Everyone has a responsibility to ensure total consent from their partners. This is one of the reasons learning about consent is so important—not being taught about consent properly doesn't excuse us from not doing it properly.

There's a certain idea of what sexual assault looks like or feels like—often based on things we've seen in the movies or the news. This is an idea of sexual assault as violent or aggressive, often featuring a stranger attacking another person. And of course, that version of assault does happen. But it isn't how sexual assault most frequently happens. Sexual assault can happen with people we know, like, trust, or sometimes even love. In fact, in around 80 percent of sexual assaults, the person who was assaulted knows the person who assaulted them (RAINN 2019).

The point of talking about this isn't to scare you, but to help you be aware that the total consent approach applies to *all* people in your life—not just the new person trying to pick you up at a party. We need to ensure that everyone—whether a stranger or a friend, partner, or date—is treating us with respect. You always have a right to control the who, what, when, where, why, and how of sex, and you deserve to have that right respected—no matter what.

Just because you know someone well doesn't mean they don't have to communicate with you safely about consent. No one gets a free pass on skipping consent. If you're ever with someone who thinks those rules don't apply to them, know that in those moments you don't have to be polite just because they're a friend or someone you know. You can firmly and clearly tell them to stop, and leave, without worrying about being rude.

Sometimes it can feel much harder to firmly set boundaries with someone we know and like than with a stranger from whom we have nothing to lose if they're upset with us. It's also harder because our brains don't like to go against what we already believe—which is known as *confirmation bias*, like we mentioned in chapter 3. This means that our brains generally like to look for information that supports what we already believe. If we've already decided that we like and trust someone and that they're unlikely to hurt us or treat us badly, then when unsafe behavior from this "safe" person starts to emerge, we have more trouble recognizing it for what it is. Our brains want to stick to what we already believe about this person. We would like to continue believing that someone we trust wouldn't hurt us, and so we can miss signs and signals that something isn't okay.

How can we better notice this type of situation and make efforts to protect ourselves if we see it happening?

Prevention Best Practice: Looking for "The Switch"

We're going to look at a three-step strategy you can use to keep yourself and others as safe as you can in sexual situations: recognizing when an interaction has become potentially dangerous, setting and communicating boundaries, and being assertive.

Research shows that the best way to prepare for a moment like this is getting familiar with something known as *the switch* (Rowe, Jouriles, and McDonald 2015; Senn et al. 2017). The switch is the moment that a healthy, consensual interaction switches to a pressured, unsafe, or coercive experience. This can be difficult to notice without some practice in thinking about it ahead of time. It can be hard for our brains to realize that we're switching from a vulnerable place of trusting someone to having to defend or assert ourselves—unless we have practiced this skill.

We often believe that when another person asks or pushes for something, they must really need it. We think it must be an important or a reasonable request and we should therefore comply with it. It's often reasonable to meet these requests in a regular social interaction. We've learned to use this approach to keep social situations running smoothly and to keep conflict to a minimum. It's often the strongest natural response our brain has when we're under pressure. But even though it's what we've been socialized to do in other situations, that doesn't mean it's what we should do, especially when it comes to sex.

Just like we can go to the gym to build certain muscles, we can build up the assertive part of our brain, too, by practicing with imagined scenarios. We need to teach our brains that this social expectation doesn't apply in sexual situations. We don't have to just say yes to a request—even if saying no causes tension or ruins the flow of an interaction. This can take practice. We started exploring how to do this by communicating our boundaries in chapter 4, but we're going to look at it more deeply here.

A leading clinical psychologist in consent, Lorelei Simpson Rowe (Rowe, Jouriles, and McDonald 2015), has a virtual reality training called "My Voice, My Choice," where participants train to look for the switch. Remember, the switch is when an interaction turns from a trusted person suggesting something sexual to that same trusted person pressuring you, trying to talk you into something, or trying to change your mind. This isn't true consent. As we practice thinking about these moments, we can train ourselves to notice the switch—when a safe person turns into an unsafe person—in real life too.

In a normal interaction, you might tell someone that you aren't interested or aren't ready for something, and that person might be a bit sad, but they listen and respect it, and you might do something else together or go your separate ways. But when the switch happens, when you tell a person that you aren't interested or don't want to do something, that person begins pressuring you, showing anger, pleading, or trying to talk you into something when you've already said no.

These moments often happen really quickly, so it helps to have your brain ready to look for certain signs and signals. If we think about it ahead of time, we can increase our ability to shift quickly from viewing a moment as normal to being able to protect our own safety if needed.

Only Asking Once

The first and most important thing to look for is very simple: a person should only ask you *once* if you're interested in doing something sexual with them. If they ask through words, body language, or both, and you say no or show signs of hesitation, discomfort, or you're quiet, then they should stop. They should not ask again. They should not try again. If they do, tell your brain to say this one thing to yourself—"*there's the switch.*" When you notice the switch—the moment that person hasn't listened or respected you the first time you said something or gave a signal—tell yourself this right after: "*You don't have to be nice.*"

Your body and brain may give you signals to smooth things over or not be assertive, like they're trained to do in another type of interaction with this person. But you can learn to override those initial signals, because they don't apply to sexual intimacy. We can start to train the brain to know and understand that you don't have to be nice in those situations. Even if the middle-floor Survival House responses we looked at in chapter 3—like freeze, appease, tend, or befriend—start to arise, you can notice those, too, and use the mantras we developed in the beginning of chapter 4 to regain control and find your voice.

Know that you have every right to say no, assertively and confidently, to anyone, including a trusted person or friend. You can get up and walk away without explanation. You can leave the room, party, or house without having to say why. You can call a friend and not worry about seeming rude if you're on the phone. You can repeat yourself as many times as you like without having to worry about sounding like a broken record. You can say, "I'm not interested, I said no" as many times as you need to, even if the other person is trying to get you to say something different or is telling you that you're overreacting. You can excuse yourself to the bathroom, lock the door, and call someone and not have to care what the other person thinks. You have every right to do what *you* need to do. Give yourself full permission to act in whatever way you need to if this other person hasn't listened to you.

And if the person gets mad or acts like you're being ridiculous instead of listening, respecting, and caring about why you're upset, this confirms that the switch has flipped, and they're no longer someone you need to listen to in this moment, even if you have before in your life.

So we have three steps:

1. Notice the switch: This is any time someone asks more than once, or ignores your signals or words.

2. Remind yourself you're allowed to be assertive. Notice any middle-floor responses that might arise, and understand why those responses are there. Then, do your best to use your mantras from chapter 4 to remind yourself you're allowed and entitled to be assertive, if it's safe to do so.

3. If it doesn't feel safe to be assertive for any reason, create space from that person. Make any excuse to leave the room, reach out to someone nearby, or say you feel sick. Then get help—try to find someone else there who you can be around, or call a cab, a friend, or the police to help you.

Practice visualizing a situation like this, and giving yourself full permission to be firm, assertive, and repetitive if you need to. Play these steps out in your head. Do this imagining on several different occasions, or even role-play being assertive like this with a friend. Try it in front of the mirror and saying it out loud.

I hope from the deepest part of my heart that neither you nor anyone you know is put in a situation in which someone threatens your right to control what's happening to you. If this ever does happen, to you or anyone you know, you should understand that it absolutely isn't your fault. Assault and abuse are *never* the fault of the people who experience them.

We're going to take some time to talk about assault, what it can feel like during and after, and what to do if this happens to you or someone you know.

RECOGNIZING ASSAULT

Sexual assault often happens in ways, in places, and with people we might not have expected. And again, it can feel different than our assumptions. It isn't always violent, loud, dramatic, or even overly physically aggressive. In fact, sexual assault can happen a lot like drowning does. When we imagine someone drowning, we probably picture them splashing and flailing and yelling for help—this is how it's shown in movies. But in real life, drowning can happen silently. Someone can be swimming along when suddenly for some reason they lose control. They might be unable to get to the surface and call for help. Someone slips under the water, and we wouldn't necessarily notice it happening if we didn't know what to look for. We also might not know why they slipped under the water or why they started drowning—but what we do need to know is what to look for and how to help immediately.

This is very similar to what can happen in our brains and bodies when something sexually intimate is happening to us that we didn't consent to. We can essentially disappear inside our own bodies. That's why we need to know what to look for—those middle- and bottom-floor responses and reactions we talked about in the Survival

House in chapter 3, even if we don't immediately know why we're having them.

What It Looks Like, What It Feels Like

As we've mentioned, experiencing a sexual assault doesn't usually feel like we expect it to. When most people imagine a sexual assault scenario, they imagine being terrified or enraged (fight or flight), with big red flags of intense emotions that are clear signals that something isn't right. People imagine that they will feel shaky and scared, or infuriated—heart in throat and ready to scream, kick, or yell for help. Or they imagine that there will be violence or physical force. But this isn't always or even often how it feels.

As we learned in chapter 3, if we aren't feeling safe and we slip into the middle floor of the Survival House, the traditional fight-or-flight responses might not feel safe or accessible as a first choice— they can feel more risky, or more likely to escalate the situation with another person. So we may instead slip into freeze, appease, or tend and befriend responses first. Remember that we don't consciously choose these responses—they're a moment-to-moment calculation by both our brain and our body working together to keep us safe. We may be drawn to appease as we people-please, smooth things over, keep the other person happy (and less scary), or even offer alternative sexual acts to avoid the worst-case scenario of something that feels even more threatening.

But as we learned, sex itself is such a vulnerable act both physically and emotionally that we often don't spend long on the middle floor of the house when we feel trapped or helpless. We can slide right into the bottom floor of the house and go into the shutdown state of dissociation. Again, this response often doesn't feel like we might expect. It doesn't necessarily feel like fear or panic. It's where we feel numb and dissociated—like we're not there and not really in our bodies, and we may be just going through the motions in a robotic way (Van der Hart, Nijenhuis, and Steele 2005).

This bottom-floor experience can continue impacting us after the assault takes place too. The robotic feeling can persist. It can numb people to the reality of what happened for hours, days, weeks, or even years after an experience has occurred. The parts of the brain that code the memory of the assault are basically fragmented and sometimes disconnected from our general awareness (Campbell 2012). These changes in the brain can cause a shutdown in our ability to express or experience emotions—known as "flat affect" (Campbell 2012). (Studies, like the one done by Möller, Söndergaard, and Helström in 2017, show that most people who visit the hospital after a rape are in this state of shutdown or immobility.)

Knowing what people often feel in this situation, which is often different than wanting to run or kick or scream, can help someone understand what happened to their body. That said, whether or not someone runs, screams, kicks, or yells doesn't change the fact that having any kind of sexual interaction with someone without their consent is sexual assault. Assault is real whether it matches up with our expectations or not, and whether someone's reactions were what they would have expected or wanted them to be or not. And if someone isn't able to react the way they might've wished, by fighting or yelling, it isn't their fault.

Losing Language and Sequence

The bottom-floor shutdown response shifts your body into a state of almost playing dead, wanting to hide and disappear until the threat is gone. As this drop to the bottom floor happens and our body goes into hide mode, blood is cut off from certain areas of the brain to conserve energy and to protect us. One of these parts of the brain, called *Broca's area*, is responsible for our ability to put thoughts and feelings into words. While we still feel all sorts of emotions on the bottom floor of the house, we might not be able to describe them. We might not be able to put words together, mumbling or staying silent instead (Van der Kolk 2013, 43). Remember, language is most accessible on the top floor of the Survival House, where we're calm and in control. It's very far away from where we're at on the bottom floor.

Broca's area is also responsible for our sense of what things happen in what order—the sequence of events (Van der Kolk 2013, 45). When we go into shutdown, our brains can't always sequence the order in which things happened without language, so we might only remember a jumbled mess of emotions, sounds, feelings, and images, with a lot of black spots in between (Van der Kolk 2013, 195).

It's important to know that if you experienced something traumatic, it's normal to not remember everything in perfect order, and to instead remember information in snapshots, pictures, sounds, sensations, and smells, rather than in words. If you experience a sexual assault and you can't find words to describe what happened, or don't feel like you remember all of the details or what happened and in what order, this doesn't mean what happened wasn't significant and important. You can still go get help. You don't have to have it all figured out, nor should you expect to right away—you just have to know something happened that didn't feel okay.

Physical Responses

Another thing that can happen during a sexual assault that can be confusing or upsetting is that the body may actually respond with arousal or even orgasm during an assault. This does *not* mean that the person who was assaulted actually wanted it, that it was okay, or that it wasn't assault. Sometimes our bodies respond to physical stimulation even if we don't want them to—the same way that we might laugh when we're tickled against our will. This reaction isn't a cause for shame or embarrassment. It can be very normal, and it doesn't mean the person who was assaulted did anything wrong. Sexual intimacy still requires consent—no matter what.

It's Not Your Fault

If you've experienced sexual assault, know that it wasn't your fault. However you reacted—whether it was freeze, appease, tend and befriend, shutdown, or something else—know that you did the best you could at the time, and that's all anyone can ask for. Even though we're learning proactive ways to cope with and prevent sexual assault, if you weren't able to, it still isn't your fault. Your brain was making moment-to-moment calculations at the time, and it did what it needed to for you to get through it.

Be gentle and compassionate with yourself, and know that you deserve help and support and there are people out there who will believe you and support you through this situation. As soon as you feel ready and able, reach out and try to talk about what happened with someone that you trust—whether a friend, family member, mentor, teacher, or professional. You are worth it.

AFTER AN ASSAULT

The hours, days, weeks, and beyond after a sexual assault can be confusing in many different ways. There is no right or wrong way to cope—everyone does the best they can in an incredibly difficult and complicated situation. But to reduce the fear and confusion, it can be helpful to know about some of the things that someone might experience after a sexual assault. (Remember that these are just *some* possible reactions—if someone doesn't have these particular reactions, their experience is still valid, real, and important.)

Cognitive Dissonance

No one wants to experience sexual assault—we don't want to have sexual assault as part of our identity or to have a survivor label as a constant reminder of what happened. So if we experience an assault, our brain might fight the reality of what happened. Our brain might find reasons why "it wasn't a big deal," try to tell us that maybe we really did want it, tell us we're just overreacting, or employ other strategies to avoid accepting what truly did happen.

Our brain wants to rationalize the experience without the label as a way to try to keep us safe. This is called *cognitive dissonance*— when we're presented with a reality in our lives that goes against what we believe to be true. We don't want to accept that we experienced a sexual assault, so we try to find a way to make it "not count." This can delay our ability to get help or tell someone what happened, but it can be a very normal reaction to have.

Know that not telling someone or getting help right away doesn't mean that what happened to you was okay. Trust your gut. Even if your head is trying to talk you out of something, if your stomach feels weird or if you feel gross or ill after a sexual experience, think back and see if all the steps of total consent were actually present. If not, tell someone safe what happened and talk it through if you can to help make sense of everything.

Emotional Reactions

Someone might feel irritable, tired, angry, or depressed after an assault. They might have nightmares, flashbacks, or startle more easily and have flight-or-fight reactions, like anxiety. Many people withdraw and isolate to cope, but many people also try to cope by being around friends, parties, or other distractions more than before.

Someone might also experience more emotional reactions to daily, seemingly normal situations than before. These new sensitivities are often in response to things that remind someone of the feeling of not being in control. For instance, being too pushy with a suggestion for a school project, a moment with a parent that feels controlling, or anything that makes someone feel even a little bit trapped or helpless can bring up intense emotional reactions.

If you notice anything out of the ordinary in yourself or a friend, consider seeking support to help navigate what you're going through.

There are no wrong answers—but the feeling of being out of control can sometimes be eased by taking control of your emotions through things like counseling and therapy.

"Tend and Befriend" and Beyond

For many people, it can be very confusing when the tend-and-befriend responses from the middle floor of the Survival House actually extend beyond the moment itself. They can make you feel an urge to stay in contact with the person who assaulted you, or even to still be friendly, nice, or flirt with them. This can be one of the most confusing responses to sexual assault.

Remember that this reaction is a result of evolution, developed to ensure our survival. When we think of humans living in small groups throughout history, even if there was a scary or threatening person in the group, we had to make the group work for our survival as a species. There weren't a lot of other options, and we needed to live in groups to survive. So often, even in the present day, the idea our brains are acting from is that if our social relationships are repaired, even after something as awful as a sexual assault, the risk of that person attacking us again in the future is reduced.

If you find yourself acting in any of these ways, or staying in touch or staying friendly with the person who assaulted you, know that it's not a sign that a sexual assault was okay—it doesn't mean that you consented, enjoyed it, wanted it, or gave permission. If you recognize this in yourself, and you would like to remove the person from your life but don't know how, speak to a trusted person or counselor to help you work through this situation safely.

Reclaiming Power

Some survivors might be hesitant about being sexually intimate again. Most people tend to expect this reaction after a frightening experience. But, other survivors might instead find an increase in their sexual activity after an assault. This can be a way for people to reclaim the feeling of free choice and control over their sexuality and sexual experiences.

Some people might feel confused about this reaction. But it's a common way that many people cope. If you find yourself in this situation, understand that your body is trying to reclaim power and control, and you don't need to feel any guilt or shame about it. You're doing the best you can to cope with a difficult situation you shouldn't have had to experience. If you decide you want help with managing your reactions or coping tools at any point, you can always reach out for help.

Getting Help

If you don't know right away what you may want to do in terms of legal action after an assault, there are some steps to keep your options open in the future. One is to have physical evidence gathered. This is typically done in an exam called a rape kit or Sexual Assault Evidence Kit (SAEK), performed by a specially trained health professional. Physical evidence of what happened is extremely helpful if you do end up choosing to take legal action at some point in the future (though collecting evidence in no way obligates you to take legal action). But this exam does need to be done fairly immediately after a sexual assault.

If you don't know right away what you may want to do in terms of legal action after an assault, there are some steps to keep your options open in the future. Physical evidence of what happened is extremely helpful if you do end up choosing to take legal action at some point in the future—and collecting evidence in no way obligates you to take legal action. Evidence is gathered in an exam called a rape kit or Sexual Assault Evidence Kit (SAEK), performed by a specially trained health professional. It needs to be done fairly immediately after a sexual assault.

It's hard to not follow the impulse to shower or clean yourself right after an assault, but if you can go directly to do the kit, the results are better. Try to have the exam before taking a shower, and avoid using the restroom, combing or brushing your hair, changing your clothes, or cleaning up any areas involved in the assault if you can. Know that even if you *have* done any of these cleaning activities, though, you can still have the exam performed.

You can get an exam at a local hospital or health clinic, or call a local Sexual Assault Hotline for direction. You don't have to be sure that an assault happened to call the hotline. Just ask them some questions—there will be no judgment, just support. The hotline can tell you what to expect during an exam. And remember, you don't need to report a crime to have the exam done or after you have it.

All of the information that the hospital or the hotline collects is confidential (again, unless there is a duty to report in the case of ongoing or public safety concerns). Know that it's also your choice whether or not to have the exam, and if you choose not to, the assault still isn't your fault. Choosing not to do a kit doesn't mean that you are saying that what happened was okay.

Long Term

Many people find that opening up to safe friends, family, or other survivors is a huge source of support for them as they navigate life after a sexual assault. Beyond that, there are lots of options for treatment of trauma from a sexual assault. Some of the best trauma-focused therapy and treatment approaches that are available right now include eye movement desensitization and reprocessing (EMDR), sensorimotor therapy, somatic experiencing, and neuro-feedback approaches. Try to find a therapist who specializes in a few of these approaches if you're ready and able to seek professional help. If you're interested in understanding these therapies further, do a quick online search to learn more about how they work.

If you don't want to talk about what happened to you, even with a professional, know that you don't have to. It's always your right to disclose or not disclose any information. But I do want you to know that there are therapies out there that can help you if you're struggling with low moods, emotional control, nightmares, or flashbacks. The therapies listed above help reintegrate your painful memories. You won't forget what happened—but these treatments can help you remember them without feeling overwhelmed, anxious, or sick.

Talk to a health professional, guidance counselor, or helpline in your area that can direct you to resources that might be available to you. You can also check out the book called *Getting Past Your Past* (Shapiro 2012), which can help you get started in understanding how therapy might be helpful to you.

While we've been discussing strategies for taking care of ourselves, there's also something we can do to help other people who might be in danger of sexual assault. This is often referred to as *bystander intervention*—stepping in to help someone if you see they're in trouble.

BYSTANDER INTERVENTION

While we've explored and talked about many ways to stay safe ourselves—likely on top of the information you already know about staying safe (such as watching your drink, not accepting drinks from strangers, going out with a group of friends and not leaving each other alone, telling someone where you're going and when you'll be back if you're going on a new date, and staying aware of your surroundings and not being distracted by your phone or music when walking)—we can also help make sure others are safe.

You can help as a bystander—someone who is present or watching something happen—in a moment you see something that doesn't look right (Hamby et al. 2016). If you see someone being asked multiple times to do something sexual after they've already said they aren't interested, go over and help them. Back them up, and tell the person to leave them alone if you feel it's safe to do so.

If you're not sure about your own safety if you stand up *directly* to the aggressor, create a distraction to take the person in trouble out of the situation if you can—you might ask them to join you outside, or help you order pizza, or that you need to talk to them privately about something in another room—anything to help them take a break from the situation so they can think about what they want to do next.

If you see anyone who looks like they're intoxicated being led away from a party or group by another person, try to intervene and check that they're okay! They're not in a position to consent to anything sexual. If you don't feel safe intervening in the situation by yourself, call a friend or family member for help, or an emergency helpline or service to ask for assistance in stopping a sexual assault.

Here are four principles (four Ds) to help you remember how you can help someone else in these situations:

- You might **distract** the person who's harassing someone with conversation or redirection to something else going on in the room, like a game—something to reduce the tension and change the dynamics so that the person in danger can get away.

- You might **delegate**—tell someone else to go get help while you keep an eye on the person in trouble, or tell a nearby authority such as a security guard or bouncer.

- You might be **direct**—if you feel safe to do so, tell the person to back off and leave the vulnerable person alone. Tell them that what they're doing or saying isn't okay. You might also directly ask the person in trouble if they're okay or how you can help, or let them know how you would like to help.

- Lastly, you might also need to **document**—record video or audio of what's happening if you're able to. This could be used as evidence in case it's needed in the future. Make sure that the person in trouble decides what they want to do with the documented information (don't take it upon yourself to make that decision for them—for example, don't share it on social media).

You can also talk with your friend group ahead of time about bystander intervention. Ask your friends to support you if you notice someone needs your help, and to keep an eye out for things that don't look right or safe.

Lastly, privilege can play a role in the ability to help in these situations. In our society, cisgender males (people who identify with the male gender they were assigned at birth), being privileged, are often particularly effective at intervening and having other people listen to them. If you're a cisgender male, you can use your privilege for good to help keep people safe when you see that a person's consent isn't being respected.

Wrapping Up

We've come so far and covered so much in this book! We stepped back and explored the bigger picture of who we are and what we want, remembering that our worth and value are a priority in every situation. We've looked at the myths around sexual intimacy and consent, debunked ideas that don't line up with healthy consent, and looked at healthier and safer methods of communicating and understanding instead.

We covered what legal consent is, as well as the basics of healthy, true, freely given consent with the HOT SPICE principles—honest, ongoing, talked-about, specific, present-moment, informed, change-able, and enthusiastically affirmative. We also looked at ways to ask for consent, as well as verbal and nonverbal signs of "yes" and "no."

We then explored why getting affirmative, enthusiastic consent is so important—because expecting our partners to say no before we stop proceeding isn't the same as getting consent. We learned how "just say no" can be a dangerous baseline to use when we look at consent because of the way our brains and bodies are wired, using the Survival House as a model. In looking at how our threat responses work in moments of consent, we learned how to better understand our own reactions as well as those of our partners, ensuring that we truly do have enthusiastic consent from everyone involved.

We also explored how to watch for second- and bottom-floor responses from the Survival House, as well as how we can set ourselves and our partners up to feel the safest and most comfortable to truly communicate our feelings. These approaches help us reduce each person's risk of feeling trapped, helpless, or rejected—which are the biggest triggers that can make us feel unsafe and interfere with healthy, mutual consent. Now that we know what to watch out for, we can work to create safe environments.

We examined our own boundaries, how to set them and express them to a partner. And then we learned how to deal with rejection and disappointment when things don't work out the way we hoped they would. We made sure we understood the dynamics of a healthy relationship that enables healthy consent—trust, communication, and respect.

We then headed off to more deeply understand both the setup and the moment of intimacy with a partner. We explored the four aspects of safety—legal, emotional, social, and physical. As we built our understanding of how to set up a safe situation, we looked at the importance of ongoing communication and the slow progression of intimacy.

As we rounded out our knowledge of what true and total consent is, we also looked at how consent can evolve over time with partners and with longer-term relationships. We talked about how drugs and alcohol can affect consent, and we learned about our rights and choices around safe sex and contraception.

We took a look at what to do if things go wrong. We learned what it can look and feel like if a sexual assault happens, both during and after the fact. And then we learned about the importance of getting help, and what that might look like. And we learned that it isn't someone's fault if a sexual assault happens to them, and that if this has happened to you, that you are worthy and deserving of support and understanding, no matter what. Lastly, we looked at how to make our world a better and safer place through bystander intervention.

We all need to work together to make things better, and this can truly start with you! Think about sharing what we've covered about consent, communication, and safety with your social groups and beyond. Not everyone might have access to this kind of information, and it can help keep people safe. By spreading this knowledge, you can help our world be a safer place. Lend this book, and tell people about it! The more we know, the better we can all do. Consent is empowerment—and we all deserve to feel respected and empowered and have healthy sexual lives.

Thank you for reading and learning about real and true consent and healthy relationships. I'm so glad we got to spend this time together, and I'm so excited for you to feel empowered, aware, safe, and in control as you explore this part of yourself and your life.

Cheers,
Cheryl M. Bradshaw

Acknowledgments

First and foremost, I want to thank *you,* as the reader of this book, for caring about consent and taking the time to truly learn about it and understand it. You will help change this world, for the better. Every person whose life you are part of will benefit from you being a part of their journey. Thank you.

I also want to thank the forerunners of trauma work, who inspired much of the content of this book and helped create a better understanding of consent and communication. Thank you to the pioneers of trauma research and their respective works: Dr. Stephen Porges (2017), Deb Dana (2018), Dr. Bessel Van der Kolk (2014), Dr. Richard Schwartz (1997), Dr. Francine Shapiro (2017), Dan Siegel and Tina Bryson (2012; 2015)—your ideas came together to shift and change how we think about sexual consent.

Thank you to New Harbinger, for taking the leap and publishing in the consent space—a daunting task, to say the least. This was a book we wanted to make sure was done right, and for that reason, it took a bit more work than usual. For that, I thank my acquisitions editor, Elizabeth Hollis Hansen, for overseeing the work on this complex and important project. Thank you also to Vicraj Gill, my editor, for the (many) back-and-forths it took to get the final product off the ground. And for the final polish to make the book what it is today, thank you to my copy editor Cecilia Santini, for all the work it took to make everything just right.

I also want to thank my late agent, Arnold Gosewich, for his ongoing support, (many) phone calls and emails, and for helping make sure I felt supported and educated through every step of this process as an author. You will be greatly missed, and I feel lucky to have known you and worked with you. Rest in peace, and thank you for everything.

I want to also thank Kristina Neuman, who created the images you see in this book. As they say, a picture is worth a thousand words, and these pictures really help bring the whole thing to life.

And of course, thank you to my parents, Mary Ann and Michael, for teaching me about consent and healthy sexuality from an early age. Without the positive foundation you provided, and the openness and healthy communication we were able to have right from day one about this kind of topic, I don't think this book would be a reality today. You really helped make it happen.

And lastly—but never leastly—a huge thank-you to my husband, Andrew, for your emotional support along every step of the way with this book. As you know, this book was the toughest one to write to date, by far. Your calm patience and steady encouragement helped me get through all the ups and downs—I couldn't have done it without you.

Additional Resources

VIDEOS AND OTHER EXAMPLES

- Head to the New Harbinger website, http://www.newharbinger.com/44499, for additional vignettes I've written to accompany this book that will help you test your knowledge of consent.

- Head to my website, http://www.cherylmbradshaw.com, for information about online resources, the video-series course that accompanies this book, and speaking engagements on the topic of consent.

- There is an excellent four-video series by Planned Parenthood that can be found at this link on YouTube: https://www.youtube.com/playlist?list=PL3xP1jlf1jgJRkChw VOlwQcV0-UqcWiFV.

   These videos are titled "How Do You Know If Someone Wants to Have Sex with You?"; "When Someone Definitely Wants to Have Sex"; "When Someone Isn't Quite Sure If They Want to Have Sex"; and "When Someone Doesn't Want to Have Sex: What Is Consent?"

   They show short vignettes and conversations between partners that can help bring some of these examples to real life. Check them out!

PROGRAMS AND SEXUAL ASSAULT PREVENTION TRAININGS

There are some excellent programs already out there that are getting some real and amazing results in helping people. Have a look at some of these resources:

- **"Flip the Script" (also known as EAAA),** by Dr. Charlene Senn, is a twelve-hour evidence-based sexual assault resistance program for first-year female university students. http://sarecentre.org

- **SafeDates:** An evidence-based curriculum intervention to help prevent emotional, physical, and sexual abuse in teen relationships. https://www.hazelden.org/web/public/safe datesproduct.page

- **Shifting Boundaries:** An evidence-based curriculum that aims to reduce dating violence and sexual harassment for teens. https://preventipv.org/materials/shifting-boundaries

- **Green Dot:** Curriculum and trainings separated by grades K–3, 6–8, 9–12, and for colleges and communities, aimed to reduce violence. https://alteristic.org/services/green-dot/

- **Coaching Boys Into Men (CBIM):** An evidence-based program that trains high school coaches to teach young male athletes healthy relationship skills and not to use violence.

- **Bringing in the Bystander:** An evidence-based workshop that helps increase awareness and motivate bystander intervention by people who may witness sexual assaults.

https://cultureofrespect.org/program/bringing-in-the-bystander

SUPPORT FOR SEXUAL ASSAULT SURVIVORS

- **National Sexual Assault Hotline (US):** 1-800-656-HOPE. There is also an online chat available at http://www.rainn.org.

- **Love Is Respect.org (US):** Get support at 1-866-331-9474, or chat at www.loveisrespect.org, a resource to empower youth to prevent and end dating abuse. A project of the National Domestic Violence Hotline.

- **Kids Help Phone (Canada):** A 24/7 national service offering professional counseling, information, referrals, and volunteer-led, text-based support. Call 1-800-668-6868 or chat at https://kidshelpphone.ca

- **Rape Crisis England and Wales:** Search here to find your local help line or chat support. https://rapecrisis.org.uk

BOOKS

- Domitrz, M. 2016. *Can I Kiss You? A Thought-Provoking Look at Relationships, Intimacy & Sexual Assault*. Milwaukee, WI: Awareness Publications.

- Lang, J. 2018. *Consent: The New Rules of Sex Education*. Emeryville, CA: Althea Press.

- Orenstein, P. 2016. *Girls & Sex: Navigating the Complicated New Landscape*. New York: HarperCollins.

- Orenstein, P. 2020. *Boys & Sex: Young Men on Hookups, Love, Porn, Consent, and Navigating the New Masculinity.* New York: HarperCollins.

- Zaloom, S. 2019. *Sex, Teens, and Everything in Between: The New and Necessary Conversations Today's Teenagers Need to Have about Consent, Sexual Harassment, Healthy Relationships, Love, and More.* Naperville, IL: Sourcebooks.

ARTICLES

Here are a few articles that expand on different ideas around consent that you may be interested in reading more about.

- Blair, J. 2016. "Women Do What They Need to Do to Survive." *Hazlitt.* http://hazlitt.net/feature/women-do-what-they-need-do-survive

- Rosenberg, T. 2018. "Equipping Women to Stop Campus Rape." *New York Times.* https://www.nytimes.com/2018/05/30/opinion/women-stop-campus-rape.html

- Vrangalova, Z. 2016. "Everything You Need to Know About Consent That You Never Learned in Sex Ed: What It Looks Like, What It Sounds Like, How to Give It, and How to Get It." https://www.teenvogue.com/story/consent-how-to

- Wong, D. 2016. "7 Reasons So Many Guys Don't Understand Sexual Consent." *Cracked.* http://www.cracked.com/blog/how-men-are-trained-to-think-sexual-assault-no-big-deal

Works Cited

Abma, J. C., and G. M. Martinez. 2017. "Sexual Activity and Contraceptive Use Among Teenagers in the United States, 2011–2015." National Health Statistics Reports, Number 104, June 22. Retrieved from: https://www.cdc.gov/nchs/data/nhsr/nhsr104.pdf

Bloom, S. L., and B. Farragher. 2010. *Destroying Sanctuary: The Crisis in Human Service Delivery Systems.* New York: Oxford University Press.

Brown, B. 2012. *Daring Greatly: How the Courage to Be Vulnerable Transforms the Way We Live, Love, Parent, and Lead.* New York: Gotham Books.

Brown, B. 2015. *Rising Strong.* First edition. New York: Spiegel & Grau.

Byrd-Craven, J., B. J. Auer, and S. M. Kennison. 2015. "Sex Differences in Salivary Cortisol Responses to Sex-Linked Stressors: A Test of the Tend-and-Befriend Model." *Adaptive Human Behavior and Physiology* 1: 408–420.

Campbell, R. 2012. "The Neurobiology of Sexual Assault. National Institute of Justice." Webinar. https://nij.ojp.gov/media/video/24056

Centers for Disease Control and Prevention (CDC). 2019a. "Hepatitis B." https://www.cdc.gov/vaccines/pubs/pinkbook/hepb.html

Centers for Disease Control and Prevention (CDC). 2019b. "PrEP." https://www.cdc.gov/hiv/basics/prep.html

Dana, D. 2018. *The Polyvagal Theory in Therapy.* New York: W. W. Norton & Company.

Domitrz, M. 2016. *Can I Kiss You? A Thought-Provoking Look at Relationships, Intimacy & Sexual Assault.* Milwaukee, WI: Awareness Publications.

Gottman, J. M., and N. Silver. 1999. *The Seven Principles for Making Marriage Work.* New York: Crown Publishers.

Government of Canada. 2019. "Hepatitis A Vaccine: Canadian Immunization Guide." https://www.canada.ca/en/public-health/services/publications/healthy-living/canadian-immunization-guide-part-4-active-vaccines/page-6-hepatitis-a-vaccine.html

Hamby, S., M. C. Weber, J. Grych, and V. Banyard. 2016. "What Difference Do Bystanders Make? The Association of Bystander Involvement with Victim Outcomes in a Community Sample." *Psychology of Violence* 6: 91–102.

Killermann, S. 2017. "The Genderbread Person." https://www.genderbread.org/.

Lang, J. 2018. *Consent: The New Rules of Sex Education.* Emeryville, CA: Althea Press.

MacLean, P. D. 1990. *The Triune Brain in Evolution: Role in Paleocerebral Functions.* New York: Springer.

Maltz, W. 2001. *The Sexual Healing Journey: A Guide for Survivors of Sexual Abuse.* New York: HarperCollins.

Möller, A., H. P. Söndergaard, and L. Helström. 2017. "Tonic Immobility During Sexual Assault—A Common Reaction Predicting Posttraumatic Stress Disorder and Severe Depression." *Acta Obstetricia et Gynecologica Scandinavica* 96: 932–938.

National Cancer Institute. 2019. "Human Papillomavirus (HPV) Vaccines." https://www.cancer.gov/about-cancer/causes-prevention/risk/infectious-agents/hpv-vaccine-fact-sheet

Porges, S. W. 2017. *The Pocket Guide to the Polyvagal Theory: The Transformative Power of Feeling Safe.* New York: W. W. Norton & Company.

RAINN (Rape, Abuse & Incest National Network). 2019. "Perpetrators of Sexual Violence: Statistics. United States, National Organization." https://www.rainn.org/statistics/perpetrators-sexual-violence

Rowe, L. S., E. N. Jouriles, and R. McDonald. 2015. "Reducing Sexual Victimization Among Adolescent Girls: A Randomized Controlled Pilot Trial of My Voice, My Choice." *Behavior Therapy* 46: 315–327.

Cheryl M. Bradshaw, MA, is a registered psychotherapist working in private practice, and author of *How to Like Yourself*—a self-esteem guide for teens—and *The Resilience Workbook for Teens*. She has been featured on various television shows, radio shows, and podcasts, including *Breakfast Television*, Global's *The Morning Show*, CBC Radio, and *Today's Parent*. Her first book was also selected as a 2016 Foreword INDIES finalist for the 2016 Young Adult Nonfiction category. In addition, Cheryl received the inaugural Outstanding Alumni Award from Yorkville University in 2017. Bradshaw served as a counselor at both Sheridan College and the University of Guelph. She also has a background in teaching, and continues to work with and volunteer with schools and charities to talk about youth and young adult mental health, self-esteem, and also to support parents with their teens.

Bradshaw resides in Hamilton, ON, Canada; with her husband, Andrew; their daughter; and their dogs, Baxter and Kiara. Find out more about her at www.cherylmbradshaw.com, and on social media @cherylmbradshaw.

Schwartz, R. C. 1997. *Internal Family Systems Therapy*. New York: Guilford Publications.

Senn, C. Y., M. Eliasziw, K. L. Hobden, I. R. Newby-Clark, P. C. Barata, H. L. Radtke, and W. Thurston. 2017. "Secondary and 2-Year Outcomes of a Sexual Assault Resistance Program for University Women." *Psychology of Women Quarterly* 41: 147–162.

Siegel, D. J. 2015. *Brainstorm: The Power and Purpose of the Teenage Brain*. New York: Penguin Publishing Group.

Siegel, D. J., and T. P. Bryson. 2012. *The Whole-Brain Child: 12 Revolutionary Strategies to Nurture Your Child's Developing Mind*. New York: Penguin Random House.

Shapiro, F. 2012. *Getting Past Your Past*. Emmaus, PA: Rodale.

Shapiro, F. 2017. *Eye Movement Desensitization and Reprocessing (EMDR) Therapy, Third Edition: Basic Principles, Protocols, and Procedures*. New York: Guilford Publications.

Taylor, S. E., L. C. Klein, B. P. Lewis, T. L. Gruenewald, R. A. Gurung, and J. A. Updegraff. 2000. "Biobehavioral Responses to Stress in Females: Tend-and-Befriend, not Fight-or-Flight." *Psychological Review* 107: 441–429.

Van der Hart, O., E. Nijenhuis, and K. Steele. 2005. "Dissociation: An Insufficiently Recognized Major Feature of Complex Posttraumatic Stress Disorder." *Journal of Trauma Stress* 18: 413–23.

Van der Kolk, B. 2015. *The Body Keeps the Score: Brain, Mind, and Body in the Healing of Trauma*. New York: Penguin Random House.

Vrangalova, Z. 2016. "Everything You Need to Know About Consent That You Never Learned in Sex Ed: What It Looks Like, What It Sounds Like, How to Give It, and How to Get It." *TeenVogue*. April 18, 2016. https://www.teenvogue.com/story/consent-how-to

More ⏱ Instant Help Books for Teens
An Imprint of New Harbinger Publications

**THE TEEN GIRL'S
SURVIVAL GUIDE**
Ten Tips for Making Friends,
Avoiding Drama & Coping
with Social Stress
978-1626253063 / US $17.95

EXPRESS YOURSELF
A Teen Girl's Guide to Speaking
Up & Being Who You Are
978-1626251489 / US $17.95

JUST AS YOU ARE
A Teen's Guide to
Self-Acceptance &
Lasting Self-Esteem
978-1626255906 / US $16.95

**PUT YOUR WORRIES
HERE**
A Creative Journal for
Teens with Anxiety
978-1684032143 / US $16.95

**THE SELF-LOVE
REVOLUTION**
Radical Body Positivity for
Girls of Color
978-1684034116 / US $16.95

STUFF THAT SUCKS
A Teen's Guide to Accepting
What You Can't Change &
Committing to What You Can
978-1626258655 / US $12.95

◆ newharbingerpublications
1-800-748-6273 / newharbinger.com

(VISA, MC, AMEX / prices subject to change without notice)
Follow Us 🅾 f 🐦 ▶ 📌 in

Register your **new harbinger** titles for additional benefits!

When you register your **new harbinger** title—purchased in any format, from any source—you get access to benefits like the following:

- Downloadable accessories like printable worksheets and extra content
- Instructional videos and audio files
- Information about updates, corrections, and new editions

Not every title has accessories, but we're adding new material all the time.

Access free accessories in 3 easy steps:

1. Sign in at NewHarbinger.com (or **register** to create an account).

2. Click on **register a book**. Search for your title and click the **register** button when it appears.

3. Click on the **book cover or title** to go to its details page. Click on **accessories** to view and access files.

That's all there is to it!

If you need help, visit:

NewHarbinger.com/accessories

new harbinger
CELEBRATING
40 YEARS